ON THE
WARRIOR'S
PATH

Philosophy, Fighting, and Martial Arts Mythology

Daniele Bolelli

BLUE SNAKE BOOKS
BERKELEY, CALIFORNIA

Published by Blue Snake Books/Frog, Ltd.

Blue Snake Books/Frog, Ltd. books are distributed by
North Atlantic Books
P.O. Box 12327
Berkeley, California 94712

Book and cover design by Jennifer Dunn

Printed in the United States of America

Blue Snake Books' publications are available through most book-stores. For further information call 800-337-2665 or visit our web-sites at www.northatlanticbooks.com or www.bluesnakebooks.com.

Substantial discounts on bulk quantities are available to corpora-tions, professional associations, and other organizations. For details and discount information, contact our special sales department.

ISBN-13: 978-1-58394-066-2

Library of Congress Cataloging-in-Publication Data

Bolelli, Daniele, 1974–
    [Tenera arte del guerriero. English]
    On the warrior's path : fighting, philosophy, and martial arts mythol-ogy / by Daniele Bolelli.
        p. cm.
Includes bibliographical references.
    ISBN 1-58394-066-9 (pbk.)
    1. Martial arts—Philosophy. 2. Martial arts—Psychological aspects.
3. Martial arts films—History and criticism. I. Title.
GV1101.B6513 2002
796.8—dc21
                                                            2002155624
            3 4 5 6 7 8 9 DATA 11 10 09 08 07

DEDICATION

To Elizabeth Han.

Thanks to martial arts I met a woman who is far more wonderful than any ideal woman that my notoriously hyperbolic imagination could conceive. On the very first day I started teaching martial arts, she was there. Having fewer moral inhibitions than a bug, I immediately and shamelessly began courting her—my wisest decision to this date. Life has not been the same since. Every day I wake up, I look into her eyes and learn something about beauty, passion, and joy.

If martial arts had given me nothing else, meeting her would have been more than enough to justify all the hours, weeks, months, and years spent training.

Since no words are strong enough to thank you for how you make me feel, I'll keep this short and will try to make up for it with kisses and massages.

ACKNOWLEDGMENTS

The words "giving thanks" don't convey the insane appreciation I have for some of the individuals I want to "give thanks to" right now.

First and foremost, Franco Bolelli and Gloria Mattioni. They are the two people who taught me how to be who I am (even though, if forced to take the stand in a court of law, they'll probably deny any responsibility). I really couldn't have fallen in better hands. Not only two adorable parents but two masters of life. I owe them everything, and perhaps even more.

My deepest thanks to James Weddell. Several times, I have exchanged glances with special persons, but I rarely met anyone with a heart as big as his. A warrior. A brother. By looking into his eyes for a couple of minutes, one can learn about what it means to be a warrior much more than by reading hundreds of books or by practicing martial arts for a lifetime.

To my grandparents for being so damn amazing (by the way, is this the wrong time to ask for another slice of tiramisu, pleeeeeeeease, Grandma?)

To my martial arts teachers: Dominic Stefano (artist, surfer, deadhead, black belt in four different martial arts and friend; I thought teachers like him existed only in dreams), Larry Wikel, Daniel and Jonathan Wang, Tim Cartmell (who is by far the best martial artist I have ever run across), and all the others who taught me something even if just for a day (especially big thanks to Mike and Heiner from Sawtelle Judo, Jiang Hao Quan, the immortal of Monterey Park, and Paolo Antonelli). To my martial friends Roberto Bonomelli, Claudio Regoli, Dennis Jelinek, T. V. "The Terror from Vietnam," and Willard Ford.

To the memory of Shannon Richardson.

To Richard Grossinger and Jess O'Brien from North Atlantic Books.

To Richard Strozzi-Heckler, who's my long-lost twin.

To anyone who ever smiled to me.

To Alessandra Chiricosta e Bruno Dorella. To Pietro, Aronne, and Rocco.

To Andrea "Babbo" Zingoni.

To Tom and Alexa Robbins (I love you guys. Without doing anything but being yourselves, you remind me of the way I want to live).

To Ray "Running Bear" Allen.

To Julio Pérez and Daniel Guedea.

To John (or was it Li?) Schroeder.

And to Elizabeth (hey, head back to the dedication page, you greedy bastard, you already had your share!)

PREFACE

The seeds of the present volume were planted with a book I published in my native Italy in 1996. For reasons that are well beyond my understanding, the book turned into an instant classic loved by martial artists as well as by people who could not care less about martial arts. What was supposed to be a simple translation from Italian into English soon took life of its own, and the result is what you hold in your hands at this very moment. Although I have tried to remain as faithful as possible to what was written at the time, too many years have gone by, and I have changed far too much to leave the book exactly as it was. For this reason, some chapters have been heavily rewritten while others are entirely new. To be more precise, the first eight chapters of this edition are a reworked, translated version of the original book, whereas the last three chapters are more recent creations and were written directly into English. The last three differ from the main body in that they mix the wild free-flowing style that characterizes the rest of the book with a more academic approach. This is why these chapters include citations and a separate bibliography while the others do not. Sadly, the academic world seems to think that if something is occasionally light-hearted, is not written in an obscure jargon intelligible only to four dusty scholars scattered around the world, and is not completely irrelevant to anyone's life, it is not serious work. To those scholars who hold this view, I offer my apologies, but I'm afraid I'll be forced to shake your academic coffins since I firmly believe that fun is not the antithesis of serious. Rather, fun is only the antithesis of boring. It is my sincere hope that you, my readers, can have as much fun reading this as I had writing it.

TABLE OF CONTENTS

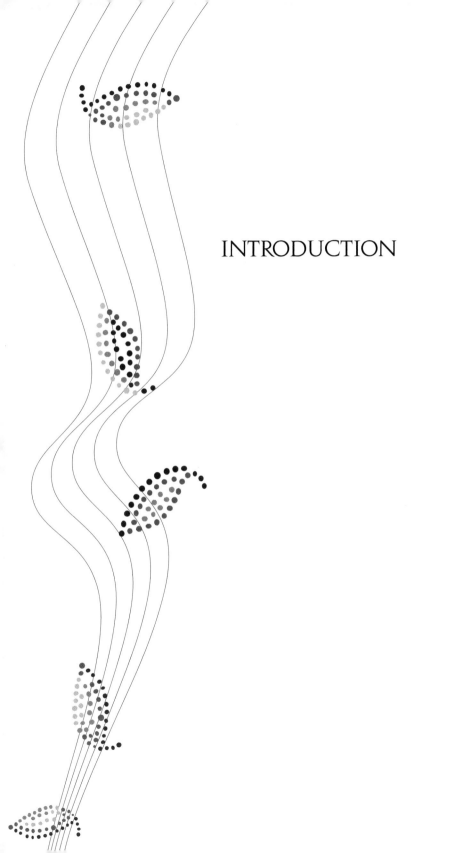

INTRODUCTION

All of the techniques handed down from my teachers appeared completely anew. Now they were vehicles for the cultivation of life and knowledge ... not devices to throw and pin people.
—Morihei Ueshiba

If you don't believe that the martial arts have anything to do with American Indian rituals, surfing, globalization, Tom Robbins' novels, the destiny of the world, the beauty of nature, and our way of perceiving reality, call my bluff—read on.

A philosophical book about martial arts is not good business. While many martial artists would rather have somebody hammering on their toes than read a book without pictures, most educated and sensitive people don't see any connection between their own lives and martial arts. But this is precisely my reason for writing this book. An unenlightened social tendency pushes us to become specialized in one, or at most two, fields and forget about the rest of the world. Brilliant scientists who don't know how to massage a beautiful woman; artists who can't run in the mountains; businessmen who don't have any idea about how to play with kids; housewives unable to shoot with bow and arrows. Restricting our horizons is encouraged in order to seek perfect efficiency in only one activity, avoid dispersing our energies, and dedicate ourselves to a well-defined career. This is how experts are born and life dies. These goals, in fact, are fitting for an assembly-line, not for human beings. Specialization is a spiritual disease—a contagious virus of the personality that is hard to escape from. It forces us to limit the range of our choices and vivisect our global vision to the point where even the most ecstatic experiences lose life and magic; it's like killing a splendid animal only to place it in a museum.

Only in the synthesis of the most diverse fields of knowledge does life reveal its full intensity. Today, in a time of globalization and collapse of national identities, this is as true as ever. The age of specialization is over. Mixing together aspects of life that have apparently little to do with each other will be the essential talent of the twenty-first century. It is time for an athletic philosophy; a philosophy forged through muscles and heart; a philosophy born out of the union of body and mind, of pragmatism and utopia, of sweet sensitivity and a warrior's determination.

Martial arts are no exception. Restricted to "insiders only," they are nothing but a ghetto. Grey. Small. Limited. No surprises. No horizons. Not a single great vision can live within its borders. Only when martial arts become part of a larger picture can we see their full potential and beauty. Traditionally, martial arts went hand in hand with acupuncture, massage, medicine, religion, and even with arts such as painting, poetry, bonsai-making, *origami,* and tea ceremonies. But these are not the only things I am referring to when I speak of a larger picture.

Rather than being confined to a separate dimension, martial arts should be an extension of our way of living, of our philosophies, of the way we educate our children, of the job we devote so much of our time to, of the relationships we cultivate, and of the choices we make everyday. I would rather have a goring match with an adult male, buffalo than advocate a new age approach to martial arts. However, fostering a holistic vision is not synonymous with the superficiality characteristic of the new age movement. A holistic approach, in fact, has been part of the true nature of martial arts for a long time. Gichin Funakoshi, the creator of *Shotokan Karate,* said that Karate is the complement to the spirit. Martial arts as something more than just martial arts. They are the means by which the character is molded and one's personality is forged. After dedicating his entire life to the practice of *Kung Fu,* Jimmy H. Woo declared, "The art of Kung Fu lies not in victory nor defeat, but in the building of human character.... Kung Fu is not important, but people are."

I don't doubt that at the dawn of martial arts, the main goal was to beat up one's opponents in the most effective way possible. But then, indirectly, the alchemy of martial arts began to strike some chords deep within the spirit of many individuals, transforming living war-machines into poets, artists, and philosophers. Certainly, the gods of martial arts had lots of fun. Like skilled magicians, they stuffed their magic hat with a fighting method, and pulled out a way of facing life: changing one's self and the world through a somatic discipline.

In martial arts circles as well as in popular culture, the concept of "the way of the warrior" is the subject of much hype. The idea underlying it views martial arts not simply as methods to break bones, but as paths for self-perfection and character-building. The word "warrior," however, is employed in so many fields, besides its original, somewhat bloody context, with so many different meanings attached to it, that it is hard to use it without sounding foolish. Yet, the sometimes misguided popularity of the "warrior" idea shows how powerful it is as an archetype. It speaks of beautiful qualities which are as rare as pygmy basketball players: a willpower that can't be broken, the discipline to transform dreams into reality, the ability to get up with one's confidence unshaken after being knocked down countless times, the commitment to fight not just for one's personal goals but for everything and everyone deserving help. The warrior doesn't simply talk about "how things should be," but acts in a way to make them happen. Being a warrior means having the strength and passion to follow one's visions.

Surfing on twenty-foot waves, or free climbing in the mountains can probably create similar results. The martial arts are a way, not *The Way*. They don't have a monopoly over the body or over the spirit. Basketball ... a drum circle ... lifting weights ... there are hundreds of possible physical vehicles for spiritual transformation. The way the Grateful Dead's percussionist Mickey Hart approaches drumming is a warrior's way. The way Phil Jackson coached the Chicago Bulls first and the Los Angeles Lakers later is as subtle and deep as the strategy of the greatest sword masters. The odysseys on foot undertaken by German visionary Werner Herzog embody the spirit of martial arts more than the actions of many martial artists. The same peak can be reached through hundreds of different paths.

Nonetheless, few things on earth deal with conflict in such a direct, touching way as the martial arts do. Contrary to other, purely verbal philosophical systems, the philosophy of martial arts is not just an intellectual endeavor, and its gifts are not gained just through reading, contemplating, talking or thinking about it. It is an athletic philosophy to be experienced through muscles and sweat as much as through the mind. Contrary to other athletic disciplines, martial arts are not simply a sport in which scoring the highest number of points defines victory, are not an art form to be appreciated merely for its aesthetic value, and are not only a skill offering the tangible gifts of strength, flexibility and dexterity.

Martial arts bring us back to something much more primal. In the fighting arts, it is our own physical wellbeing that is on the line. The fear of violence, the fear of being the bull's eye for an attack of overwhelmingly superior physical force, the fear that women, men, and animals alike feel when a stronger, meaner predator assigns them the role of the prey: these are the forces that martial arts play with. Something that everyone who ever lived and who ever will live experiences at some point. Even in a relatively safe society, even among people who probably will never have to face violence, its presence is very much alive. No matter how brilliant and sophisticated we get, in the back of our minds always looms the question of what could we do if attacked by a physical force that knows no common sense, doesn't listen to good words and can't be stopped by gentleness. From school playgrounds to abusive marriages, from dark streets at night to our very private nightmares, the theaters in which the prospect of physical conflict divides humanity into fearful prey or fighters are more than can be numbered.

The very physical nature of our existence makes it impossible to completely escape this primordial fear. Maybe we can ignore it, and maybe we can live fulfilling lives without ever having to face it. But this fear, however silent and dormant it may be, is something that always lives within us. Through practice of the fighting arts, the martial artist stares his own fears in the eyes. He challenges them every time when facing an opponent. Every fight is a battle against our own limits and weaknesses. Much like a doctor injects a disease into a patient in order to allow him or her to build antibodies and be immunized against this very same disease, martial arts use small-scale violence in order to immunize its practitioners against the fear of violence. Physical aggression, the most dramatic, obvious, and scary manifestation of conflict, is the training tool used in the martial arts to lose all fear of conflict.

The moment Fear begins to lose its grip on us, every instant of daily existence can become more peaceful and enjoyable: a fifty-pound weight being lifted off our shoulders. Only then does it become possible for serenity to come dancing into our lives. Thanks to the confidence developed through training, this serenity runs deep and cannot be easily threatened by the fear of conflicts, verbal or physical that they may be. The martial artist doesn't chat about spirituality. He or she puts it into action.

Ooops, the magic word just escaped my lips: spirituality. Many martial artists are superficially infatuated with the mystic halo surrounding their arts, while just as many martial artists label anything having to do with spirituality as mere superstition. Both factions make a huge mistake. They look at spirituality as something strange, esoteric, removed from daily life. They look at it as if it were some far away dimension wrapped in clouds of mystery and incense, something with no connection to the most mundane aspects of life. Forgetting that true spirituality is not ascetic nor against life, both its friends and its foes call "spiritual" what is remote and beyond the material world. But spirituality is just the opposite. It is the quintessence of life. It is a way of waking up, of walking, of smiling, of dancing.

Spiritual are those who are not satisfied with surviving, but want to turn daily experiences into sources of ecstasy. Under this light, the spirituality of martial arts is not the exclusive dominion of the Eastern traditions that have given birth to many fighting arts. Speaking about *Shambala* Buddhist teachings, the renowned Tibetan monk Chogyam Trungpa has a beautiful thing to say, "The Shambala teachings are founded on the premise that there is basic human wisdom that can help to solve the world's problems. This wisdom does not belong to any one culture or religion, nor does it come only from the West or the East. Rather, it is a tradition of human warriorship that has existed in many cultures at many times throughout history."

The same words could be applied to martial arts. It is not necessary to be Asian in order to enjoy martial arts, just as it is not necessary to be an American Indian in order to appreciate the power of a sweat lodge. It is Character that matters, not ethnicity. I once happened to listen to Wallace Black Elk, a Lakota medicine man, as he spoke about American Indian religion, expressing virtually the same ideas stated by Trungpa. There are things that cannot be caged within the limits of geographic or racial boundaries. They are paths open to anyone whose heart beats for something more than simple inertia.

Just as with any path, martial arts can transport people to thousands of different places. Everything depends on the destination chosen by the individual who walks along the path. Martial arts could be used for something, for nothing, or for everything. We can receive only as much water as our cup can hold. Like the genie in the magic lamp, martial arts can only give us what we have the courage to desire.

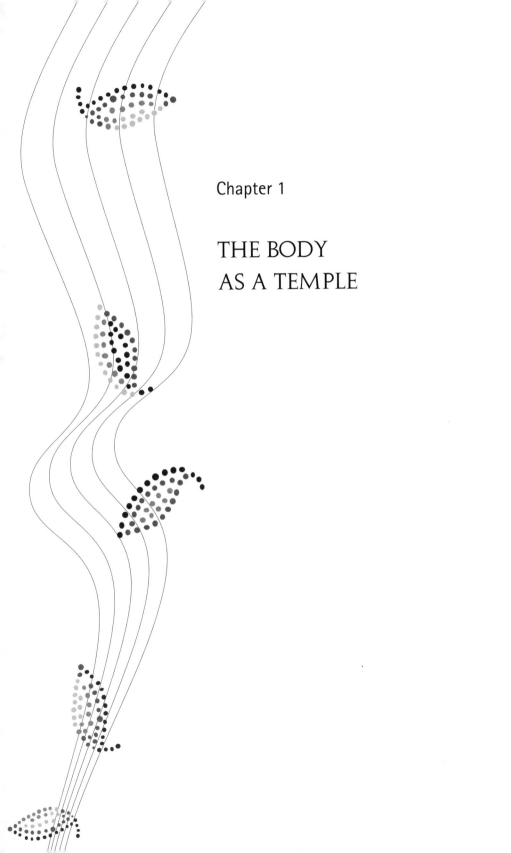

Chapter 1

THE BODY
AS A TEMPLE

... our body is a vertebrate mammal being—and our souls are out in the wilderness.

—Gary Snyder

On that day, throughout the entire Hunan province, everyone's hair had been seduced to dance in the wind. But the monks didn't need to worry about it, since they had solved the problem at the root. On the day they had embraced Buddhism, they had cropped their hair in such a way that even the storm could not threaten the order of their heads. More worrisome, instead, was the smile on the lips of their master. Nervously the monks exchanged wondering glances. Nobody could feel safe when Bodhidharma smiled. Since he had arrived from the south, that frightening Indian had already upset the spiritual life of the monks several times. His smile always signaled an upcoming emotional earthquake. What else could be expected from the man who would give birth to Zen?

As for Bodhidharma himself, he couldn't help but smile. The sight of the monks benumbed by the cold, trying to protect themselves from the bites of the wind by hiding deep within their robes, was a source of great amusement. They looked like drenched puppies. There they were—men who spent all their energies searching for enlightenment—forced by a small tempest to run for cover. Prospective holy men without the strength to resist a little chill. Their spirits were the reflection of their bodies: weak, stooped, graceless. They had forgotten that within their flesh grew the seeds of those same powers that made the deer jump in the mountains, the same powers used by tigers on the hunt and by birds in flight. They were so busy studying the sutras that they had forgotten about the sutra written in the body. How could men who walked like achy librarians dream of becoming buddhas? Bodhidharma's smile widened. He knew exactly what to do with those monks. He would give them the most extreme, unsettling Zen koan. What up until that day had been held in monopoly by drunken peasants, soldiers and ruthless bandits would become the main discipline of the temple. No more stooped monks, but spiritual warriors. A discipline forging body and soul at the same time: the martial arts. The *Shaolin* temple was never going to be the same.

Even the world would have never been the same had any of the Western prophets been struck by the same intuition that the myth attributes to Bodhidharma. Imagine Jesus Christ preaching after a session of *Tai Chi Chuan*. Probably, the entire Western culture would be drastically different. No rivalry between spirit and body. No tug-of-war between the soul yearning for Heaven and the body restraining it on Earth. Rather than wasting our energies quarreling with our bodies and with the natural world, we could let spirituality and sensuality dance cheek to cheek.

I don't think it is an exaggeration to say that most human problems have their origin in a bad relationship with the body. I agree completely with Tai Chi master Yang Jwing-Ming when he writes that the world needs *Chi Kung* as much as it needs a perfect plan for the restoration of global economy. Sociologists, politicians and religious leaders consider the confusion and stress which make up much of modern society as the result of wrong choices and lack of values. I believe the root of it all to be much deeper than that. Values and choices originate from our way of breathing. Breathing well and listening to the voice of the muscles are arts that should be taught in school. But unfortunately, no divine intervention has yet put Bodhidharma in charge of the Ministry of Education.

At the basis of our education lies a suicidal dualism. As Alan Watts wrote:

> Physical education is the fundamental discipline of life, but it is actually despised, neglected, and taught intellectually, because the true intent of our schools is to inculcate the virtues of cunning and calculation which will make money.... The establishment is a class of physical barbarians ... they do not know how to transform money into physical enjoyment. They were never taught how to husband plants and animals for food, how to cook, how to

make clothes and build houses, how to dance and breathe, how to do yoga for finding one's true center, or how to make love.

And Nietzsche, the only true poet-warrior of German philosophy, adds "... a mere disciplining of thoughts and feelings is virtually nothing ... one first has to convince the body."

We are stuck within a system which gives all the power to the mind, and just the leftovers to the body. Ahead of us lies a trap from which there is no way out. The moment they ask us to choose between two different paths, the implicit message is that we can only follow one. Either scholars or athletes. Either creative or pragmatic. But the idea that if we want one thing we must renounce something else is one of the worse aberrations ever invented. Bodhidharma knew this well. What good can come from a philosophy created by individuals with hunched shoulders and withered bodies? What good can come from individuals who have never danced under the moonlight or who have never dived into a river at dawn? An individual who is truly alive should not settle for anything less than the totality of experience.

But taking care of one's body is not enough. There are many ways of taking care of the body that are little better than not taking care of it at all. Many people who go to the gym and workout regularly, as well as many martial artists, treat their bodies as inanimate objects, as machines in need of a tune-up. They train their muscles, but they don't learn anything from the body. Taking care of the body becomes just a duty forced upon us by hedonistic, superficial whims, or by the commandments of health-consciousness. But the harmony between mind and body is something that has nothing to do with the obsession for fitness. The body is not a product. It is an experience. Physical health and strength are wonderful side effects, not ultimate goals. The real goal is not so much centered on one's physical appearance as it is about one's character. The type of physical awareness we have and the kind of relationship we maintain with our bodies influence our personality at least as much as the kind of books we read. I know people who are naturally strong, healthy and agile, but they are not aware of it. Their bodies possess a wisdom that they can't access. They are like little gnomes who direct the body from the control room; prisoners within their heads.

Having a perfect body is not nearly as important as learning how to listen to its voice. During a training session, when the rational mind slows down the flow of thoughts, the body begins to disclose its secrets. Consciousness is free to travel from one muscle to the next, and have access to powers unknown to those who can't go beyond cerebral activity. For a few minutes or for a few hours, the social identity is left behind. Our names, our professions, our ideas stop having any importance. The only thing that matters is the stream of energy flowing within us. The strength of an adult mammal, not different from that of a buffalo, a wolf, or a jaguar. A wild being aware of the life-force pulsating in every pore of the skin. This is not just a physical experience. It is spiritual. It transforms the body as well as the character.

The personality of those who know how to come in contact with this dimension changes even in everyday life, during the ordinary state of consciousness. It changes the way we move. It changes the way we speak. It changes the way we face life. When you know the intensity of that power, a halo of confidence begins to follow you in every moment. There is an incredible difference between those who experience their power only through the mind and those who also feel it in the body. A person who knows there is a wild wolf living under the skin has less reason to be intimidated by reality. The body becomes a source of confidence. Through the body it is possible to discover an inner strength that can help us overcome practical as well as spiritual limits. Even when the power of the mind is in doubt, the body can provide tangible proof.

In martial arts everything begins with the body. First, one gets acquainted with it, and slowly becomes intimate with it. The body is transformed into the best ally of the spirit. Then spirit and body become one. The sensorial windows are cleaned until they shine.

During a fight there is no time to analyze. Suddenly we are immersed in a situation where rational thinking has less credibility than an invitation to have lunch with a cannibal tribe. Being projected into this dimension is exciting and scary at the same time. It is a space where everything that we have been taught in school doesn't matter at all. Neither logic nor intelligence can help us. Too slow. Stopping to think is out of the question. Everything happens faster than the brain can possibly register. Panicking, the mind leaves as soon as it realizes that it can't do anything to control the situation.

At this point the wisdom of the body starts dancing. The intensity of the training sets off the alarm and the five senses jump out of their lethargy. Like antennae, they capture every signal traveling through the air in order to polish some fractions of seconds off our reaction times. Instinct guides our reflexes to act even before we know what is happening. A punch cuts through the air and the body moves away from its trajectory. But if the body is not receptive, the fight is over in a second.

Remembering his experience as a *judoka,* Mickey Hart likens the martial artist to a tiger: "Have you ever looked into a tiger's eye? What immediately grips you is that the tiger is right there— all four hundred and fifty pounds focused with gleaming maximum attention on you. No distractions, no hesitations, just a calm powerful contemplation." Being one hundred percent present here and now is the talent of a true martial artist. Through the practice of martial arts, we can learn to feel this presence, call upon it, cultivate it, make it a part of ourselves. When we can enter this dimension at will, it becomes possible to have free access to an enormous source of power. It is like having an inner button. In any situation you can find yourself in, touch the button and ... BOOM! You are there, alive, aware, full of energy, with total intensity and concentration. All distractions disappear in the twinkling of an eye. A second before, fatigue and weakness were upon us; the next moment we are the center of high voltage energy: from Clark Kent to Superman even without the aid of the telephone booth. It is not a metaphor or an exaggeration. Anyone who has experienced it knows what I am talking about.

Because of the physical nature of martial arts, we can't lie to ourselves. There is no need for somebody to tell us whether we are moving mechanically or are truly present. When you are there, you know it. Every gesture serves as verification of our feelings. But the martial applications are just one of the thousands of methods in which this power can be applied. Once you know how to push the button, you can do it at any moment, inside or outside of the *dojo*. No need to be intense twenty-four hours a day. The energy is always there within reach. It is a fire that doesn't always burn in the open, but under the skin the coals are always lit. Anyone sensitive enough can feel the vibration. As soon as you enter in a room, right away you perceive who is an individual from head to toe and who has never listened to the voice of the body.

Those who have never approached their bodies as temples have no idea of what they are missing. The frog at the bottom of the well sees only a fraction of light and believes it to be the whole sky. The same happens to those who have lost the address of their bodies. Life happens around them but they don't realize it. They see and feel only the things that are noisy and excessive. Dull, catatonic perceptions. Maybe somebody put Prozac in their vitamins when they were children. On the other hand, their minds are always hyperactive, too caught up in the unstoppable flow of thoughts to pay any attention to the ecstasy dancing in front of their noses. Like somnambulists, they don't even realize they are prisoners of their sleep. They don't know what it means to live in a body that doesn't just serve as a machine carrying the mind from one place to another. Even the ability to love and to feel loved is limited if the perceptions are dull. The martial arts are one of the methods that can teach the body to reawaken the sleepy senses. Those smart enough not to put them back to sleep at the end of the training see their everyday life filling up with magic.

There is no need to travel to exotic places, load up on drugs, or drive one hundred miles an hour in order to feel alive. It is not necessary to look for particularly strong sensations, because when the five senses are awakened, every sensation is a strong one. The scent of the earth after a summer storm. The embrace of a lover. The vastness of the sky above. Small experiences that could travel through our consciousness without leaving any trace become the messengers of a beauty that cannot be measured. A few days ago I saw a duck being born into a flower pot. Nothing exceptional. Nothing momentous. Just the first moments in the life of a duckling. But I spent almost an hour watching, absorbed by the scene. People kept walking by, oblivious to what was happening literally under their noses. I couldn't help but smile. Perhaps they wouldn't have taken notice even if a Greek goddess had been dancing tango between the flowers. Their perceptions were not ready to register anything but the strictly indispensable. Always in motion. Always in a hurry. Traveling under the protection of a glass-bell transporting them from home to the office and isolating them from the surrounding sensorial world. Beauty sacrificed on the altar of efficiency. A sad waste of potential.

But if you stop long enough to listen, the body tells you all you want to know. A sensitive body gives back to life its natural intensity. Whether it is the presence of a wonderful sunset or a danger waiting behind the corner, you feel it immediately. Ten manuals on the psychology of behavior cannot teach what a single glance can reveal. The body of a person is the greatest imaginable source of information. Look at people for thirty seconds and intuitively perceive what their friends have learned after years of acquaintance. Reading body language is not the result of practice, nor is it a technique that can be taught. It is something that happens naturally when mind and body don't fight each other. Like dreams, intuitions are meant to be felt, not interpreted. Whether aware of it or not, every individual emanates a particular vibration. All the experiences of a lifetime, all the emotions a person has ever felt are tattooed on the skin. The quintessence of a person is revealed in every gesture. A dog only needs a few seconds sniffing people to decide whether to snap at them, ignore them, or jump on their legs wagging its tail. Damaged perceptions are the only reason why humans need more time. It is not magic—it would be insulting to think that a Chihuahua is more magical than we are—it is just a matter of opening one's eyes.

When I am in balance, I can meet total strangers and know much about their lives before we are even introduced. I look into their eyes and it is like reading an open book. Sometimes it is not even necessary to see. Someone is talking behind me and the tone of their voice is enough to tell me what kind of person I am dealing with. In the course of time, my intuitions have been confirmed so many times that it would be silly to dismiss them as coincidences.

But this is not a good reason for inflating my ego. In fact, I refuse to consider this as my personal ability. Anyone paying attention to their perceptions can do the same. Five senses working together give birth to the sixth. Seeing the heart of a person never seemed to me something exceptional or in any way magical. The only thing surprising to me is that there are many people who can't do it.

But maybe I shouldn't be so surprised. Maybe it is not strange that people who willingly decide to spend a third of their days locked in an office, devoting themselves to activities for which they often have no passion, lose the ability to "feel." Maybe it is not strange at all. A poor awareness of one's body is the symptom of a deeper illness: physical, spiritual and social at the same time. Like a martial artist who has developed an exceptional technique, but who doesn't have the wisdom to know when to use it, Western culture has in its hands the technological potential to turn the planet into a paradise, but has no clue as to how to enjoy it. Rather than being used as means to enrich our daily lives, the evermore sophisticated technological inventions become a way to take us further away from our bodies and our nature.

In an age of virtual reality, world wide web, and increasing dematerialization of work, the assiduous practice of the martial arts could seem useless and anachronistic. But maybe today, even more than in the past, disciplines like martial arts are essential. We no longer live in a society where in order to bring food home, a man has to rely on his own speed and muscles to hunt buffalo and run for miles in the forest. Today many people spend eight hours a day sitting before a computer or behind a desk, forcing their bodies to an unnatural stasis. Overworked minds, inert bodies. Depending increasingly more on an immaterial form of technology, we confine the body to a subordinate position. We grow detached from it. We forget its magic. We forget its power. The imbalance between our virtual self and our physical self grows every day.

In this context, martial arts could be a way to reverse this tendency, or at least to limit the damage. During practice, the rational mind takes a rest. Even in the middle of a big city, after many hours spent overworking the brain, we can discover again the wild nature of the body and feel the energy of life pulsing in the muscles. Martial arts used as an antidote against the secession of the mind. Many techniques of meditation try to achieve the same results, but often they rely on a relatively passive way, involving the body only marginally. In this way, since relaxing becomes a mere mental effort ("Now I must relax.") rather than a natural, physical process, they end up producing more paranoia than harmony. On the contrary, what martial arts point out is that individual harmony can only begin with one's body.

However, martial arts are just an oasis in the desert, an isolated voice running against the currents of mainstream society. This situation is not just the result of having adopted a sedentary way of life, but is also the effect of the domination over the collective psyche by philosophies and religions that appreciate an abstract metaphysics better than the physical nature of experience. We don't need to look far to see the signals. It is enough to turn on the radio or the television. In the media, the body is shown mainly through negative images: the blood of the victims of a terrorist attack, a graphic report showing the effects of deadly diseases, the feelings of prisoners sentenced to death at the moment of the execution, scenes of devastation from a country torn apart by war, the decay of undernourished children. We are reminded of the body only when it hurts. It is portrayed as a source of suffering, as a negative entity giving people pain and trouble.

As an alternative to the idea of "body-equals-pain," the media offer other images of the body that are perfectly complementary to the first—as an expensive machine, a work of craftsmanship, a luxurious commodity, nothing but a market product. If you don't like it, you can always change it with plastic surgery. If your engine is losing its power, just add a pacemaker. Whether for health or for aesthetic reasons, nonetheless it is the external intervention of technology that resolves all our problems: this is the implicit message that we hear on a daily basis. There is no awareness in the body, and it is definitely not seen as a part of us. It is barely more than the clothes we choose to wear for the day. Something that we can always transform according to the current fashion (granted that we have enough money to afford it). This is what happens when for too long people put their trust in transcendent philosophies.

Centuries of Aristotle, Plato, and Descartes have bulldozed the way open to the decay of the body. The majority of our planetary culture has been indoctrinated to perceive both Nature and the body through the lenses of a mechanistic vision of reality; Descartes' "*cogito ergo sum*" ("I think therefore I am"), identifying our selves only as a function of thinking, thereby turning the physical world into a barren wasteland. We have chosen to follow Kant along the road of "progress" and science rather than sitting around the campfire with Gary Snyder and riding with Black Elk in the Prairies. Big mistake. In Gary Snyder's own words: "Otherworldly philosophies end up doing more damage to the planet (and human psyches) than the pain and suffering that is in the existential conditions they seek to transcend."

Perhaps even more than the dogma of scientific philosophies, the gloomy ghost of many different religious doctrines planted the seeds for the rejection of the body. Doctrines of renunciation according to which life is a sin to be amended.

Doctrines born out of the fear to be truly alive. In their eyes, the Earth is nothing but a vale of tears, a place of suffering, nothing more than an obligatory stop on the way to reach better destinations. The body is a heavy burden pinning us to the ground, an obstacle on the way to Heaven. Not only are body and soul not in harmony, but they are antithetical principles at war with each other. The natural pulse of a healthy body is considered a source of dangerous distractions. But penitence, mortification and self-repression are the virtues of those who got burned by fire once, and since then have chosen to stay in the dark, of those who don't have the courage to say yes to life, of those who have no eyes to appreciate the dance of the nymphs or ears to hear the beating heart of a forest.

Neglecting the body as if it were an enemy is the first step towards opening the door to the worst kinds of aberration. A spiritual and ecological destruction has bloomed from the seeds of this school of thought. If the Earth is nothing but a place of transition given to us for our use, why worry about treating it fairly? A few millennia under the tutelage of these religions have left a very heavy mark: deforestation, rampant pollution, sexual repression, atomic bombs, indiscriminate destruction of other peoples and other species.

Chogyam Trungpa's words hit the target.

> When human beings lose their connection to nature, to heaven and earth, then they do not know how to nurture their environment or how to rule their world—which is saying the same thing. Human beings destroy their ecology at the same time that they destroy one another. From that perspective, healing our society goes hand in hand with healing our personal, elemental connection with the phenomenal world.

Philosophies, religions, and bad habits have embedded themselves so deeply that most people can't find a way to connect with the body anymore. Sometimes they try in rough and often counterproductive ways, through pain and masochistic disciplines: hurting oneself in order to feel alive. But this is only the other side of the physical repression they are trying to escape. There is no harmony or beauty in this search, only desperation.

What we need is something else—a way of cleansing the character of the junk we have drowned it in, a way to remind us that the body is not a prison, but a sacred temple that cannot be bought by money or accessed by technology. Turn your body into a temple and nature starts talking to you. It brings you back to a wilder, more authentic state. Nature is not just a name to identify what we have not yet covered with concrete and asphalt. It is life lived without fear, without sense of guilt; life not enslaved by the artificial rules of a society which has lost its center. People talk much about ecology and the need to slow down the crisis of the global ecosystem, but there can be no solution to the problems of nature unless we can find nature within. And we can't find our own nature without passing through the body. The healthiest, most ecological and spiritual act that we can perform is to rediscover the energies of the body. A man who knows that body and spirit are part of each other doesn't need anyone to remind him that he is alive, nor does he have any reason to upset the ecological balance. Only the sky above his head and the earth under his feet. His body is the only home. It is the only thing that never abandons him, the only one that truly belongs to him. Such an individual is a threat to every form of established authority. A wolf that can't be tamed. He is not under anyone's orders and doesn't accept dogmas because he already has within himself everything he needs to face life. When streams of power flow in the veins of your body, dependency on external factors is reduced to a minimum. Confidence follows your every move, and thus it is a pleasure to be surrounded by animals, mountains, and trees, since you don't have the feeling of being in a hostile environment. It is a splendid, thrilling experience. Pure euphoria. I pass the ball to Werner Herzog: "My steps are resolute. And now the Earth shakes. When I walk, a buffalo walks. When I rest, a mountain rests." This is echoed by Zen master Dogen, "If you doubt mountains walking you don't know your own walking."

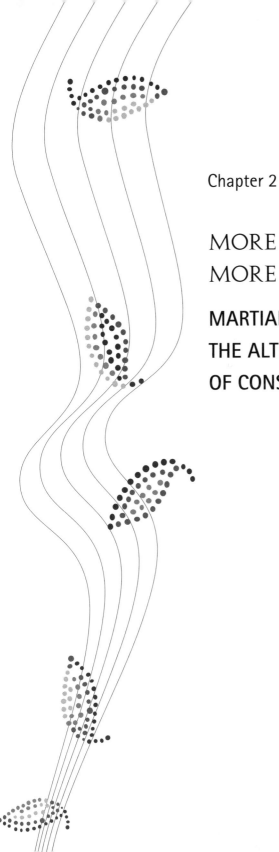

Chapter 2

MORE THAN MARTIAL, MORE THAN ART

MARTIAL ARTS AND THE ALTERATION OF CONSCIOUSNESS

Archery is, therefore, not practiced solely for hitting the target; the swordsman does not wield the sword just for the sake of outdoing his opponent; the dancer does not dance just to perform certain rhythmical movements of the body. The mind has first to be attuned to the Unconscious.

—D.T. Suzuki

The journey begins by going within. The inner chemistry of our body is a mine full of surprises. Both scientists and mystics agree that the majority of human beings utilize only a fraction of their genetic potentials. Most people live at a comfortable distance from their bodies. Since they pay hardly any attention to them, their senses are dull and can only perceive the most obvious stimuli. As humans, we spend so much time inside our heads that we often forget the way out. We are in the same condition as retarded baboons trying to play a grand piano. Our equipment is simply much too sophisticated for us to know what to do with it. Our bodies are the kingdoms of lost continents and unknown lands. Columbus, Livingstone, Stanley, Marco Polo, and Neil Armstrong are just Boy Scouts compared to the explorers of the inner space. The first step to unlock the doors of perception and sniff the scent of the Secret is to awaken the five senses from the numbness that normally surrounds them.

When the senses wake up, people talk about altered states, but actually nothing about them is altered. The only real alteration is the sleep into which we often let them fall. Bringing them back to life is the only natural thing we can do. It is as if we defined the starting of an engine as an "altered state" only because we consider normal leaving it turned off. The fascination many people have for "supernatural" phenomena is the result of their lack of deep knowledge of what Nature is about.

There are many ways that can bring us close to caressing the skin of ecstasy: the artist consumed by the fire of creative passion, the sound of tribal drums taking one far beyond the borders of rationality, the ascetic's mortification of the body, tantric sexuality, shamanic rituals, falling in love, the adrenaline-soaked trance of competition, the narcotic caresses of hallucinogens, Jerry Garcia celebrating on stage the last edition of the Eleusinian Mysteries, listening to the voice of the woods at sunset, dancing until you forget who you are and only the dance remains. And naturally the martial arts. Ecstasy is not a faraway, unreachable dimension. It is right here, just a few feet away from the sleep of the senses. As William Blake put it; "If the doors of perception were cleansed, everything would appear to man as it is, infinite." The miracle of ordinary reality is revealed to those who have eyes to see it and ears to hear it.

There are substances, words, actions, and experiences that can shake our senses out of their lethargy. Although it is true that hundreds of different methods can lead us there, it is also true that many of them require tremendous efforts, or a complex organization. Some depend upon events beyond our control, while others are just temporary shortcuts that can project us in space for a few hours but can't change our everyday consciousness.

Martial arts are one among the many means to come in contact with our perceptive potential. During the practice of martial arts we go back to a primordial simplicity. No need of drugs, objects, or external substances to help us. We are left alone with our bodies. We don't have to wait for things to happen; we make them happen. It is like Zen archery or like climbing mountains: we use the body as a take-off runway for inner skies. The more a martial artist is in tune with his or her body, the more effective he or she will be. By chiseling away fractions of a second from their reaction time, by sharpening their reflexes, by learning to feel the subtle changes in the opponent's balance and intent, martial artists begin to listen to the voice of the senses. The very physical nature of training forces them to do so. If wise enough not to leave these newly acquired skills in the dojo, martial artists will then be able to use the "awakened" senses to experience subtler states of consciousness in the midst of everyday life.

An obvious objection has just found its way in my head stopping me before I jump into an adoring exaltation of the martial arts. If it is true that martial arts grant free access to the dwelling of ecstasy, why do the faces of most martial artists look like what Blake had in mind when he wrote, "He whose face gives no light, shall never become a star"? As much as I love martial arts, I am not so crazy as to think that practicing them is enough to overcome all the limits of one's personality. It is also true that the connection between the expansion of consciousness and martial arts is less evident than what I may have so far suggested. No, I haven't lied. The connection is there, and potentially is under everyone's eyes. But in order to find the treasures of martial arts, we have to know what to look for. One can spend a lifetime practicing martial arts without ever seeing the vastness of horizons they can open. Many people wouldn't see a diamond if it were shining in their faces. Since every person has a different character and different expectations, everyone will end up finding different answers in the martial arts. I am sure many martial artists would have less trouble roasting their mothers than seeing any connection whatsoever between expanded states of consciousness and martial arts. But if we opened our eyes and minds, we could save Mom and store her in the fridge for another occasion. Psychedelic states (by which I don't mean any drug-induced escape from reality but rather the natural expansion of our perception of reality) and martial arts can easily walk hand in hand. Bodhidharma and Timothy Leary find out they are twins separated at birth.

Internal martial arts such as Tai Chi Chuan, *Pa Kua, Hsing-i,* and *Aikido* speak the language of the psychedelic body. What is more psychedelic, in fact, than the ability to feel how an opponent will attack before a single gesture is made? What is more psychedelic than an Aikido master so in control of his inner energy as to smile softly while two Schwarzenegger clones try in vain to move him? Or what about the notion of Chi, the invisible energy which gives life to all creatures? Chi, outlaw Taoist wanted in vain by the inquisition of Western science; the breath of a God forgotten in a mortal body; nightmare of the laws of physics; Zen warrior of our will; fuel in the engine of the universe.

Few things are as psychedelic as the concept of Chi. All internal arts are based on the development of an energy that cannot be seen, touched, or perceived by any of the senses. To the ears of the fundamentalists of science, the descriptions of Chi sound like a mystical heresy, the supernatural invention of a vivid imagination. The nature of Chi is elusive. No scientific instrument has ever managed to capture it. Like the true Tao, Chi can be perceived, but not analyzed in a laboratory. According to internal martial artists, acupuncturists, traditional Chinese doctors, shiatsu masseurs, Chi is anything but supernatural. It is something used on a daily basis in order to make their arts effective. Chi is as natural as our blood and our breath. Just as blood and breath, Chi has its own circulation, a boundless source of energy for anyone who learns to tap into it. Despite what some people think, power is not in the barrel of a gun (sorry Mr. Mao), but inside us. According to its fans, potentially our Chi can do more than any technology.

Science rejects what it cannot explain, whereas according to religion any experience beyond the limits of our understanding is an incontestable proof of the existence of God (if we have awakened in a good mood) or of the Devil (if the day has started on the wrong foot). Personally, I don't believe in Chi, nor do I disbelieve it. By nature, I find beliefs of any kinds to be cheap. Ultimately what I believe, or don't believe, doesn't really matter. The only thing that beliefs do for me is close my mind to different possibilities. As far as Chi goes, the world of martial arts is unfortunately filled with charlatans who make a living fabricating wild stories about Chi powers. However, that doesn't mean that the whole notion of Chi should be dismissed as a fantasy.

So often I have witnessed things I would have never believed possible that I am more than willing to keep my mind open to the idea that our bodies are home to forces that we don't fully comprehend. My definition of impossible has been overrun by external events so often as to take away from me any certainty regarding what is possible and what is not. Once, for example, during a performance, a martial arts teacher exposed his throat and asked me to strike him with my best shot. A few inches before I made contact, my hand lost half of its initial power. It felt like trying to punch someone through water. However, at the moment of impact I still had enough energy to knock down a normal man. Had I tried to stick my hand through a concrete wall, maybe I would have had better luck. His throat felt like a close relative of the Great Wall. He smiled, thanked me, and continued his demonstration as if nothing had happened. Whether this demonstration was the result of a trick or not, I have no way of knowing, but it certainly helped me to keep an open mind.

Martial arts folklore is full of stories about deeds that make the laws of physics blush with embarrassment and about individuals who could compete with the Jedi masters of the Star Wars trilogy. For example, the ability to feel an impending attack is not the product of George Lucas' fantasy; rather it is a talent that has saved the lives of many warriors throughout the centuries. Obviously there are many more martial artists who boast of achieving these capacities than those who can actually demonstrate them in action. However, there are also cases beyond doubt, such as the tale of a Japanese *Kenjutsu* master related in the *Gekken Sodai*. The man in question was peacefully resting in his garden in the company of few of his most trusted students when, all of a sudden, he jumped up with a worried look on his face and began to search the premises expecting to find an enemy. Disconcerted at not finding any visible threat, he retired in his room. When questioned by his students about his bizarre behavior, he replied that his training had enabled him to feel an attack before it materialized and this ability had never failed him until that day. As he was resting in the garden, he had perceived the presence of a hostile force, but not having seen anything to confirm his suspicion, he was now trying to understand what had happened. It was at this point that one of his students apologized profusely saying that as they were resting in the garden, he had thought how easy it would have been to attack his master while he had his guard down. The master's feeling, therefore, had been accurate.

In the world of Chinese martial arts, there is a kung fu style which is the perfect synthesis between fighting efficiency and alteration of consciousness. Powered by free-roaming intuition, it is the perfect discipline for a martial artist who fell in a barrel of tequila as a child and ascended to the dimension of alcoholic nirvana. It is the Drunken Style. In one of the many versions of the myth, the legend tells of a martial artist who, despite his great ability, couldn't improve anymore. Although he trained very hard and tried in every way to learn his master's lessons, he had reached a plateau. All his effort seemed in vain. No land in sight. One night, frustrated by his failures, he went to a tavern and started drinking without restraint. While he was occupied with emptying bottles, some of his classmates went to tell the master that they had seen him dishonoring their school by getting drunk in public. Furious, the master immediately went to the tavern ready to teach him a hard lesson. But the tutelary deities of intoxicated states had a surprise for him. The drunken student defended himself with amazing ability. Free from the bondage of his rational mind, he moved with natural grace. Anytime he seemed to be about to lose his balance, he recovered at the last possible instant and counterattacked in unpredictable ways. Being unable to follow the irrational strategy of that alcoholic dance, the master was defeated. Once he was sober again, the student realized he had created a new kung fu style. Far from being an open invitation to ask for the bottle's help before training, the Drunken Style tries to bring its practitioners to a spiritual condition free from the mind's obstructionism. If the Fool of the Tarot were a martial artist, he would practice the Drunken Style. Quick changes of rhythm and direction aim at surprising and confusing the opponents. The unstable fantasy of the Drunken Style undermines the enemies' mental schemes. Opening, closing. Yin, yang. The Drunken boxer must continually move between different states of consciousness: from the euphoric lightness of intoxication to the lucidity necessary to counterattack at the right moment. It is constant change with no breaks. If the fighter is too rational, he becomes predictable. If he ventures too deeply into alteration, he loses precision. The effectiveness of the Drunken Style's physical applications depends on the constant alternating between extremes.

A relatively recent, more reliable example of the seemingly supernatural perceptions achieved via martial arts training can be found in the creator of Aikido, Morihei Ueshiba. Trying to explain why it was so hard to hit him, even for a sword-wielding opponent, Ueshiba declared, "It was nothing. Just a matter of clarity of mind and body. When the opponent attacked, I could see a flash of white light, the size of a pebble, flying before the sword. I could see clearly that when a white light gleamed, the sword would follow immediately. All I did was avoid the streams of white light."

Easy, right? Not just seeing, but having visions without any aid from Albert Hofmann's chemical creations. Being so in tune with one's perceptions and so centered in oneself as to be able to feel the most subtle vibrations of ordinary reality: seeing the invisible, feeling what we cannot know. Clearly this is not the result of a day or a year spent practicing martial arts. There is no "easy, quick method to become a Jedi master in ten simple lessons." The development of talents unknown to normal men is a path that takes years and that only very few individuals can follow.

However, it is not necessary to ascend to the Olympus of martial arts in order to discover their perception-expanding potential. A popular view holds that the alteration of consciousness through martial arts is a mysterious, esoteric phenomenon reserved only for the greatest masters of the internal arts. Nothing could be further from the truth. We don't need Ueshiba's visionary ability to see that in the hands of a decent teacher almost any type of martial art can become a vehicle for the expansion of consciousness. The ability to use our bodies to move at will between different states of consciousness is used from the time we take our first step in a martial art school. For example, during a fight, when the adrenaline starts dancing on our skin, it is of vital importance to regain the calm and clarity of mind to face the situation. Breathing deeply makes it possible to control the flow of adrenaline and allow us to regulate our internal chemistry. The very simple action (simple in theory, that is) of remaining relaxed in the midst of tension and chaos is an example of manipulating the consciousness, which most decent martial artists get a chance to eventually experience.

Maintaining calmness under attack, however, is not the only way to play with one's emotions in order to obtain an edge during a sparring session. Letting the adrenaline explode could be equally effective: with a barbaric roar and lightning in the eyes, we become the incarnation of fighting furor and let our energy overwhelm the opponent. The emotional mood in a martial arts school can change so rapidly that it is vital for fighters to move their consciousness to fit the situation. One moment the room could look like a Tibetan monastery on a quiet day as the martial artists try to cleanse their minds and let go of unnecessary tensions, and the next second, once the sparring begins, it can be transformed into a temple dedicated to the gods of war.

There are moments in which I would rather have a head-butting match with a mountain than continue training. For example, few things in the world can climb to the top ten of pain and boredom as much as being forced for a long time in a horse stance (*ma bu* in Chinese: one of the most common stances used in nearly all martial arts). Used as a training device for standing meditation and for building good alignment, the horse stance is what the legs see in their worse nightmares. It is the torture chamber of the quadriceps. I have to admit that seeing great psychedelic potentials at a time when your legs are ready to apply for an early retirement and your mind is wandering trying to find something to distract it from pain may not be easy. However, the psychedelic potentials are there, and we don't have to be masochist to see them. In order to resist for a long time, we have to be able to move the mind somewhere else. Beyond the body, beyond the sharp teeth of Pain. We can keep on suffering stoically during every workout, any time that the hated horse stance comes around, or we can use it to learn to move our consciousness at will. Pain and fatigue exhaust the body until the rational mind, not the least intrigued by all of this, decides to take off and leave us free to explore other states of consciousness. At this point we can really begin playing. Without a mind reminding it of its limits, the body discovers new sources of energy. It doesn't obey the commands of rationality any longer, but dances to the rhythm of a natural sensitivity. It begins moving under the guide of a different kind of wisdom. We do the right thing without even thinking. No trace of fatigue is left.

However, all these examples are nothing but a few drops in the ocean. It is like being in the center of a huge mandala. The center is our body and all around there are hundreds of different martial arts styles, each composed of thousands of techniques which pave the way for just as many internal destinations. Whether we decide to just scratch the surface of martial arts, or we go straight to their hearts, depends only on our open-mindedness. We certainly don't lack the paths, and all we need to travel is right here within our own bodies.

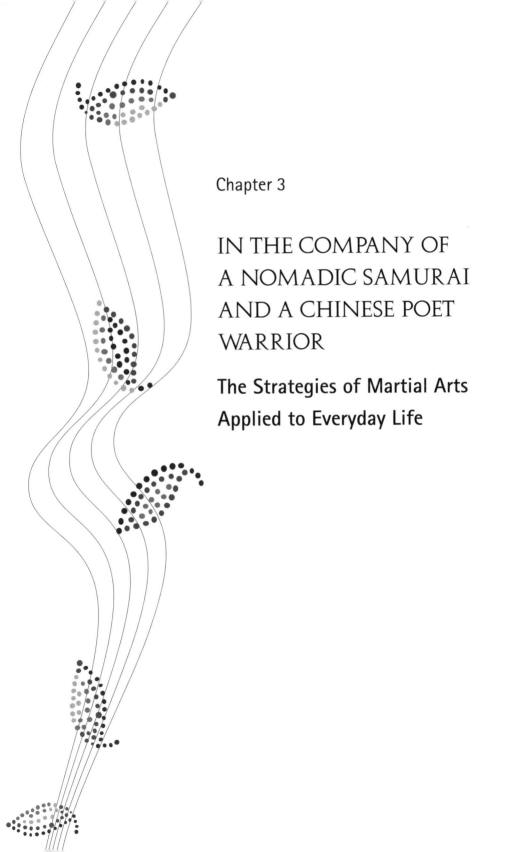

Chapter 3

IN THE COMPANY OF A NOMADIC SAMURAI AND A CHINESE POET WARRIOR

The Strategies of Martial Arts Applied to Everyday Life

He is not the ideal candidate for the Nobel Peace Prize. He is not exactly the kind of man that you would like to see asking for your daughter's hand. Maybe we could overlook the mean gossips telling us that he has never seen a bathtub up close, and maybe we could even ignore that his idea of small talk is a graphic description of severed heads and streams of blood. However, some problem may arise if he decided to test his sword's edge. They say he skipped classes the day when at school they taught compassion. Had he earned a friend for every foe he defeated, he would be a man surrounded with affection. But friendship and love have never been his playmates. The highlight of his curriculum between the age of thirteen and thirty was his duels against sixty different swordsmen. Sixty men who after meeting him were not going to contribute to the overpopulation of Asia. No, definitely he is not one of Gandhi's disciples. He is Miyamoto Musashi, one of the most famous samurai in Japanese history.

The other man who knocks on our door today is very different. His name has been a legend for more than 2,000 years, but the story of his life is wrapped in mystery. We have a name, *Sun Tzu,* and some fleeting description of a Chinese general who lived at the time of the Warring States. A Taoist warrior who could not be defeated on the battlefield. His strategic skill made him invincible, but unlike Musashi, Sun Tzu wasn't out looking for personal successes written with other peoples' blood, and neither did he see fighting as his only reason for living. *The Art of War,* the little book that reserved for him a place of honor in the Paradise of Martial Artists, is not a bible for war-fanatics. From the title on the cover down to the words "The End" on the last page, the book talks about war, but warfare can also be seen as barely more than a pretext for a series of lessons on how to live life. Like all good Taoists, Sun Tzu was an artist of paradoxes. The essence of *The Art of War* can be applied to warfare just as it can be applied to any other aspect of living. Musashi and Sun Tzu couldn't be any more different from each other, but both *The Book of Five Rings* by Mushashi and *The Art of War* by Sun Tzu are authentic masterpieces teaching how to face conflict in order to live beyond conflict: not simply martial arts strategy, but strategy of life.

In everyday life, conflict never leaves our side. It follows us closely at every step. Physical combat is nothing but the most spectacular and obvious form of conflict. Whether we are aware of it or not, we face several conflicts every day. Stupidity tells us that a physical combat is only physical combat and that the strategy of martial arts serves no other end but to defeat the opponent. However, a double-digit IQ is enough to understand that something much more important is at stake. Emerging as the winner out of a thousand fights and becoming gods of martial effectiveness is not such a great result if we end up being defeated by daily life. If the strategy of martial arts was only useful for martial arts, we could take *The Art of War* and *The Book of Five Rings,* drop them in the toilet and flush them (for this blasphemy, I drop on my knees begging the spirit of Sun Tzu for forgiveness. Begging Musashi for forgiveness would be pointless, so I won't even try.) Combat is a ritual form that points out to a wider conflict. For this reason, truly understanding the strategy of combat means understanding how to face reality rather than endure it. Am I saying that life is tough and mean, and we have to constantly fight in order not to be crushed? Not at all. Living life as if it were an eternal battle is not wise but only paranoid. The philosophy of martial arts invites us to do just the opposite.

Muscles relaxed and a smile on our lips. Those who understand the nature of conflict don't need to fight constantly. Sun Tzu perfectly sums up the fundamentals of the art of war by saying that those who win by fighting are not truly skilled. Truly skilled are those who win without fighting. This is the origin of the strategy of martial arts. Zhuge Liang, another famous philosopher of warfare, writes, "The wise man wins before fighting, whereas the ignorant needs to fight in order to win," and Ueshiba adds, "Solving problems before they form is the way of the warrior."

All of this clearly sounds very good, but one question begs us to stop. Even the dumbest clients of the Lobotomy Department wouldn't object to obtaining the maximum result with minimum effort, but how is it possible to move beyond theory and turn good principles into actual practice? Martial arts strategists are often stingy when it comes to detailed explanations, but on one point they all agree. Power is in the eyes. Piercing eyes to go beyond appearances. Piercing eyes to cut through the veil of mental speculations and find ourselves face to face with the essence of things. Observation and knowledge are close friends. One comes from the other. Entrusting ourselves to tarot or palm reading, interrogating the stars, and looking into the crystal ball are the subterfuges of those who haven't learned how to observe. There is no need for magicians, mediums or psychics to guide our actions. Reality has no secrets for those who can penetrate it with their sight.

A book is mysterious and unknown only as long as we try to read it with our eyes closed. It is enough to open our eyes and begin reading, and all the secrets are revealed. Reality is no different. The strategy of martial arts begins by looking around and *reading* the state of things. If more people trusted their own perceptions, priests and new age gurus would be unemployed. The ability to observe is as simple as it is rare because most people prefer believing in just about anyone else rather than in themselves. On the contrary, the martial strategist doesn't base his decisions on secondhand opinions, but chooses to look directly into the heart of things. Even more than strength and agility, awareness is our best weapon: a dynamic awareness that can look simultaneously into the present, the future, and the past.

Human stupidity is a well whose depth never stops amazing me. I receive further confirmation of this when I see the art of facing conflict used not to elevate the quality of our relationships, but as an aid to further the quarrels of managers involved in corporate battles. In the last few years, it has become fashionable among the sharks of the business world to sharpen their teeth with Sun Tzu's and Musashi's writings. In United States as well as in Japan, corporations even sponsor seminars using *The Book of Five Rings* and *The Art of War* as textbooks to learn new techniques to boost productivity and defeat business rivals. Emotionally manipulating others to obtain one's goal is a common practice among the "samurai" managers. However, they invented nothing that religious and political leaders, as well as scores of individuals we stumble upon in daily life, don't know already. They are smart enough to transform their dreams into reality, but not smart enough to truly know how to dream. Few things are worse than having talent and wasting it on the wrong goals.

Their pettiness however doesn't make them any less dangerous. When the ability to play with other people's emotions and to find the right words at the right time falls into the hands of individuals whose heart is not clean, it is as if the proverbial mad scientist found himself in control of a nuclear missiles launching-station. Sweetness and good intentions can't do anything to defend us from their attacks. Even muscles and courage don't help against those who can manipulate our minds. If we don't recognize who the enemy attacking us is, our chances to protect ourselves drop to the ground. "Reading" their heart is the only way to avoid falling into a trap.

Following the intricate dance of cause and effect, farsightedness gives rise to a 360 degrees awareness. If we know in advance in which direction the present situation can evolve, we can solve problems before they originate. In my experience, knowing how to read other peoples' intentions has helped me to face potentially dangerous situations without having to use any force. Once, years ago, I had just walked out of a martial arts school after a night of training when a huge man (or maybe he was a dwarf mountain) came toward me. His words were far from threatening. "What martial art do you practice?" was all he said, but inside of me a bell rang warning me of imminent danger. "Kung Fu San Soo," I replied. "Do you think it's effective?" he countered. Acting on pure instinct and without really knowing why, I lied. "I wouldn't know. Tonight is my first lesson, so I still don't really know anything about fighting." Apparently dissatisfied with my answer, the man lost interest in me and went to ask the same question to another martial artist who had left the school right behind me. As soon as he heard the answer, the man unleashed a punch aimed at my classmate's face. Not a good idea. His target, having no Christian intention to offer either cheek, reacted instantly teaching the giant that it is not wise to start a fight with people who spend half of their lives training for combat. After picking up the pieces of the giant (or maybe he was a dwarf mountain), my classmate told me that he already had to defend himself several times from the attacks of bullies out to pump their egos by knocking out martial artists. Not that the whole thing troubled him the least. My classmate, in fact, wasn't exactly the kind of guy who would walk out of his way to avoid a fight. Not sharing his enthusiasm for reshaping the faces and the ambitions of local bullies, I much prefer it if I can avoid the fight by recognizing in advance any sign of potential threat.

"Feeling" other people's intentions when there is no time to comprehend is not a special talent reserved for enlightened masters. Only a bad relationship with our perceptions and a poor regard for our intuition can take this fundamental weapon away from us. Centuries of strict rationalism and skeptical philosophies have contributed to undermine our natural sensitivity.

Often, the obsession for being fair and objective under all circumstances transforms our mind into a tribunal. We want tangible proofs and objective evidence to believe in what we already know. Unfortunately, intuition is not objective and offers no proofs. It travels on tracks that are much too fast to wait for the painfully slow speed at which logical analysis moves. Rational understanding arrives at the finish line hours later (if it arrives at all), only to confirm what intuition has already revealed to us. If on that night outside of the martial arts school, I had stopped to doubt the validity of my perception, the only thing I could have gained was a solid and tangible punch on the nose, or at best, I would have found myself wrestling against a pissed-off dwarf mountain.

Understanding with the heart before understanding with the mind is difficult only if we let ourselves fall prey to attacks of Cartesian paranoia. Considering intuition a talent much too essential to be sacrificed to the whims of logic, a Taoist text called *The Book of Balance and Harmony* (I guess corny titles are not the monopoly of new agers) said; "Judging and comprehending only after events take place doesn't deserve to be called understanding." The ability of martial strategists, therefore, consists in perceiving what is not yet manifest: being aware of everything around us, including what is not yet out in the open.

Martial philosophers, however, are not the only ones who can benefit from this talent. In no other field of experience, is recognizing the natural rhythm of things as important as in human relationships. Feeling the emotions of those who are in front of us before a single word is spoken puts us in the position to avoid useless conflicts. It's like entering a mine-field armed with a map showing in detail where the mines are. There is no risk of stepping on a mine by mistake. Smelling the emotional air, we know in advance when it's time to speak and when it's better to keep our mouths shut, when to be tough and when to be gentle. This is not a crash course in armchair psychology. Rather, it is the very basis of knowing ourselves and others in order to obtain the maximum result with minimum effort. The right means at the wrong time only end up producing disasters. No matter if they are animated by the best intentions, even the sweetest and nicest words create conflict and misunderstanding if spoken at the wrong time.

In martial arts recognizing the rhythm of things spells the difference between victory and defeat. If we recognize the fraction of a second in which the opponent's defense is at its weakest, an easy victory is within reach. As Sun Tzu writes, "The best commander attacks when the least skilled is still busy making plans." In this case, the parallel between life and martial arts is complete. When we seize the right moment, everything comes easy, and is resolved in the best possible way without the need to struggle. But if we don't know how to read the rhythm of things, wrong choices and useless waste of energy are always knocking on our doors. The martial artist who learns how to feel his opponent's heart within a few seconds can see what no psychology degree can ever teach you. Looking into someone's eyes and catching their essence is not the kind of experience you learn from books.

The martial artist as a master of moods. Artist of mental states. Conductor of an orchestra of emotions. Musashi wrote, "Once you understand the science of martial arts, there is nothing that you won't be able to see." Those who know in depth the dynamics of conflict can choose even when no choice seems available. The vast majority of human beings go through life on cruise control. The events of life apply leverage on their emotions, and in turn their emotions control their behavior. Emotions causing a reaction that causes other emotions causing another reaction that.... Unconscious prisoners of a very vicious karmic cycle. In this context, emotions are not the result of a choice, but of automatic responses. With the hammer, the doctor softly hits a nerve under the knee, and the leg reacts with a kick. Many people face life without any more awareness than Pavlov's dogs. Constantly manipulated by external stimuli, they end up as hostages in the hands of events beyond their control.

It's the story of the bull and the matador. Theoretically, a 600 pound pissed-off bull should have no trouble goring into space a little guy who looks like he has just come out from a visit with the tailor of the Village People. Even armed with a sharp piece of steel, in an open conflict, the matador can't compete with the bull's raw strength. But the matador has on his side a skill that turns the tables in his favor. The matador is smart (well, maybe calling smart a man who makes a living challenging cows' mates to duels is debatable, but let's go on....) The matador steps into the arena with extreme lucidity and with the help of a strategy, whereas the bull doesn't know any alternative but to charge head on following the orders of his rage. Whereas the matador acts using the emotions of his bovine foe to his own advantage, the bull simply reacts to the matador's provocations. The one winning the conflict is not the one who is strongest, but the one who knows how to control the opponent emotionally.

The martial artist does the same thing. Just as a doctor hits the right spot to obtain a particular physiological response, the martial artist touches some emotional chords, thus manipulating the opponent's reactions. Fear, for example. The Judo teacher of Mickey Hart (the drummer of the Grateful Dead) used to tell him, "People think you're crazy.... You are so intense when you fight that you scare them. Their fear is a powerful weapon. Learn how to use it." Following this advice, before the beginning of the first few matches of his career, Hart stared down the opponents with his "Mad Hun" eyes while repeating his "You're Mine" mantra. The opponents, sometimes fighters with much more experience, would fall into the trap of nervousness and forget their technical superiority, thus offering many easy victories to Hart.

Fear, however, is only one of the emotions that can be exploited to decide the fate of a match. Musashi used to irritate his opponents by purposefully arriving late to the duels. Feeding the opponent's ego by simulating weakness and giving him the impression that winning is going to be easy, can make him overconfident and careless. On the contrary, displaying a tremendous degree of relaxation and self-confidence when countering the first attacks can intimidate the opponent and take any security away from him. Annoying, distracting, or embarrassing are only some of the ways to dominate conflict by using people's emotions. Inducing a certain state of mind is sufficient to control those who don't know any other way than reacting to stimuli. The martial artist who learns how to recognize and use states of mind possesses an exceptional weapon.

However, limiting this skill to the field of combat is like having Shannon Seta's creative talent and using it to become a corporate shark. Those who know how to play with emotions and with the reactions that emotions induce are in the position to turn off the cruise control and take charge of the wheel of their life. They stop being chess pieces that can be moved by other people's actions. Free from automatic responses, they don't jump as soon as someone waves a red flag under their nose. They are in control.

Am I exalting a human model that is halfway between Hegel and Terminator? A cold, cunning, insensitive control freak who doesn't know how to be swept by passion? Am I saying that emotions are a weakness and that we should get rid of them in favor of an aseptic, robotic kind of consciousness? Of course, not. "Robotic" is always helplessly reacting to external stimuli. Widening the range of choice is the antithesis of being robotic. And this is exactly what recognizing emotions and knowing how to play with them means. Rather than being pushed left and right by other peoples' words and actions, we get to choose which path to follow. To quit being defenseless doesn't mean becoming insensitive. We simply stop being the bull whose destiny is to lose. Rather than charging blindly, we can choose how to respond. We could choose not to fall any longer in the trap of provocations, and gore the matador sending him to the Paradise of Defeated Bullfighters, or maybe we could invite him to a romantic escape in the Caribbean.

Once we find out that we are free to choose, we can become designers of our own lives. We become at the same time the artist and the masterpiece. The game begins by observing one's natural reactions to the events taking place in daily life. It is not a bad psychoanalytic trip. Rather, it is the most direct way to free ourselves from our most obvious character limitations, and be reborn in a new skin. Is there any life in what you are about to do? What effect are your words and actions going to create? Before acting, it is enough to stop for a few seconds to find out the answer to these questions in order to know ahead how we will affect the situation we are in. This is the way to learn how to win without fighting.

It is said that when two tigers fight, one will die and the other will carry deep scars forever. Head-on conflict is hardly a good deal, even for the "winner." Too much effort, and too much wasted energy. A conflict from which one person comes out on top and the other comes out defeated is the worse way to obtain the desired result. It leaves behind bad feelings and plants deep seeds of resentment: dry wood thrown over the karmic fire of rivalry and vengeance.

A famous story tells of three people wanting to cross a canyon that was inhabited by a wild horse. The horse was known for its bad attitude and fierce territorial nature. Anyone trying to cross had to face his hooves. The first of the three men was a good fighter and a great runner. As soon as the horse saw him, he charged against him, but thanks to his skill the man managed to fend off all the attacks and run across. Tired and worn out, he stopped on the other side of the canyon to see how the others would do. With great cleverness, the second man noticed a path among the rocks that run too high to be reached by the horse's hooves. He took it and arrived safely to the other side, while the horse stared at him, neighing with furor and frustration. Surprisingly, the third man didn't even attempt to follow the path found by the second. With absolute calm and ease, he just walked through the canyon. He passed by just a few steps from the horse, but the horse didn't attack. The horse simply neighed softly and let him go on his way. Creating a favorable emotional situation, the third man had obtained the same result for which the first two had to sweat.

In most tribal societies, any solution that is not born out of everyone's consensus is no solution at all. If, in order to obtain a certain result, we have to get in conflict with someone, a mistake has been made. Taoism, the philosophical soul at the roots of many styles of martial arts, views open conflict as the last choice after all others have failed. It is possible to cross the canyon without fighting. Most often, there is a way to come to terms even with the most aggressive person and to obtain a result that leaves both satisfied. Observe where they come from and try to meet them halfway to find a positive solution to an otherwise annoying situation. If they don't feel attacked and criticized, but rather they feel accepted, most people relax and suddenly open up to what we have to say.

Of course, there are also people for whom the happy ending is not an option: they are flexible like the Berlin Wall and open to dialogue like a grumpy inquisitor. Once, I had the ambiguous honor of receiving the attention of two nazi-skinheads bent on removing my head from my shoulders because they didn't like my looks. After a rapid check of the situation, my range of choices seemed quite limited. Usually, good manners don't enjoy much success with people having SS soldiers in war gear printed on their T-shirts. Also, a brawl with two guys who don't care too much about getting hurt as long as they can hurt you more is not a brilliant idea. Both gentleness and toughness would have probably done little to avoid a fight from which none of us would have walked away in one piece. Having nothing to gain from what seemed like an inevitable fight, I did the only thing that they didn't expect. Pretending not to notice their hostility, I began my best imitation of the reddest redneck on the planet. As I loudly expressed opinions that Hitler would have found a bit too reactionary, I saw the most complete confusion in their eyes. They were ready to beat up a guy whose hair was too long, and he was coming out with a series of stereotypes that made their ideology seem deep and sophisticated! Maybe for the first time in their lives, they had met someone who was clearly and embarrassingly dumber than they were. This was definitely not what they had anticipated. I continued my rap for a few minutes until the two Nazis, stunned and uneasy because of the surprise, momentarily forgot their hostile intentions. Before leaving them to their destiny, I received from the two gentlemen street directions and also managed to have them offer me some chewing gum: the best result that I could obtain from a wrong situation. If accepting a challenge is not worth it, diverting others' aggressiveness is a good way to avoid wasting energy in useless conflicts.

The psychological fencing of martial strategy, however, works only at one condition: an incredible amount of self-confidence. Think of the way Michael Jordan walks onto the basketball court. Everything about him—his way of walking, the look in his eyes, the tone of his voice—tells you that he owns the court. The game hasn't even started, but he is already dominating it psychologically. Of course it is easy to be confident when you possess Jordan's skill, but technical skill only takes you so far. There are many technically amazing players who will never be anything more than good players because they lack the power shining in Jordan's eyes. Michael Jordan, the Buddha, as well as the best warriors, all possess the same frightening self-confidence: the ability to come out as winners before a single word is pronounced or an action is taken. This skill comes from the awareness of having nothing to fear. If you don't give up your power and your dignity, no one can take it from you.

Few things can create such a deep feeling of self-confidence as the martial arts. As a martial artist, you know that if good words and gentleness fail and a good strategic ability can't avoid conflict, you are ready to openly face anything coming your way. Even if things go wrong and conflict is inescapable, it would likely be more a problem for your opponents than for you. Just like animals attack when they perceive fear and weakness, people can unconsciously feel a person's power and will probably avoid conflict with those who are animated by deep self-confidence. Without having a fighter's inner strength, it is very hard to be able to stay calm enough to offer alternative options. The offerings of peace made by a person who is unafraid of conflict carry a weight that peace born out of fear will never have. If you don't have credibility, even the best dialectical ability will not be successful. The power of a warrior to dominate conflict is the best guarantee of avoiding conflict. In order to live in peace, one needs the strength to win a war. It is not a formula that can be easily applied, or a technique that can be learned. It is what people see when they look into your eyes. It is the energy dancing around your skin. It is the person that you chose to become.

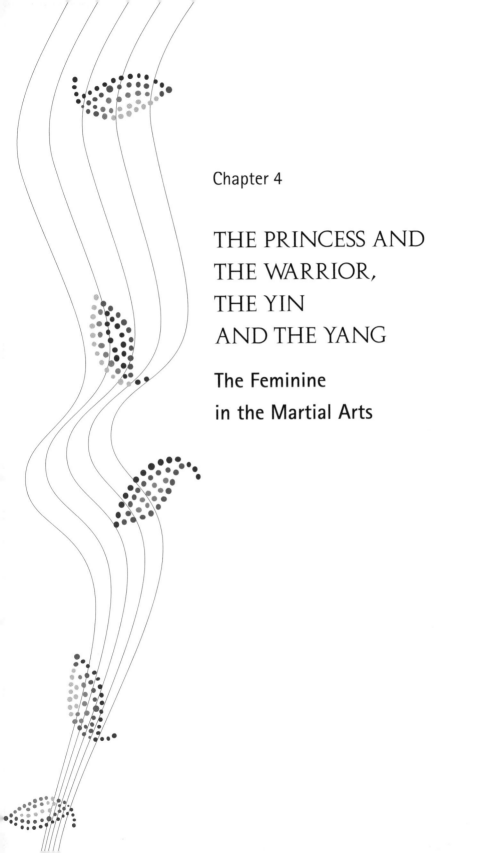

Chapter 4

THE PRINCESS AND
THE WARRIOR,
THE YIN
AND THE YANG

The Feminine
in the Martial Arts

J ust as all good old fairy tales, even this one begins with "Once upon a time.... " It is one of the great universal myths that our ancestors have told around the fire for countless generations. It is the story of a warrior who, in order to save the beautiful princess, must face the monster who captured her and who brought to a premature end the career of all the prospective heroes who tried to free her thus far. The details of the myth change in different versions and in different ages. The monster may be the dragon of medieval fairy tales or the villain of Western movies. The story has been told in hundreds of different ways, but the substance doesn't change. Whether the authors of the various versions of the myth were conscious of it or not, this story holds the key to one of the cosmic archetypes of Life's primordial energies.

What?!? Are you telling us that one of the most essential secrets of existence is to be found in the old, boring, overused, macho tale? You bet. The greatest universal myths are not passed on throughout the centuries just because they climbed to the best sellers list during the Early Paleolithic and somehow stuck around ever since. If a myth spreads through time and space, it is because it possesses something that touches the heart of human beings. Such a myth is not just any story. It is a revelation of what we could be if we had the courage to live up to our potentials. The myth we are dealing with today is not a tale reserved for wannabe warriors and prissy ladies. Rather, it speaks to all human beings.

The Warrior, the Dragon and the Princess are symbolic images of the energies that humans grapple with on a daily basis. Every living being has to face the dragon's challenge. The Dragon comes to us in the shape of all the problems we stumble upon in daily life. It is the force that constantly stands between us and the fulfillment of our desires. Our fears, our laziness, our resignation to mediocrity feed the Dragon's fire. Every time that a "I wish I could" crosses our minds, the Dragon has won.

Those who don't know how to be warriors cannot help but surrender to the problems barring their way, and are left powerless to watch their dreams being crushed. It takes a warrior to have the power and will to step up and challenge the Dragon. The hero of this story (and of countless other legends) is a warrior because being gentle and kindhearted is not enough to defeat the monster keeping us away from our goal. The Dragon doesn't move just because we say "please." The hero must be an expert in the art of war in order to win in this conflict. The hero is pure yang energy. Assertiveness, strength, bravery, an indomitable will, and the skill of a god in the midst of battle are the Warrior's tools. These are the qualities that separate him from common men. And without them, no one could free the Princess.

Whereas others renounce the challenge because they lack the courage to look at danger in the eyes, or are pushed back by the Dragon's fighting prowess and apparent invincibility, the Warrior is not afraid to step into battle and doesn't lack the martial skills to take down the Dragon. If the Warrior is a concentrate of yang energy, the Princess is absolute yin. The Princess is not a secondary character in the story, and is not simply an attractive excuse for the Warrior to show off his fighting ability. Her role is not any less important than that of the Warrior. She is everything that the Warrior doesn't have. Sensitivity, creativity, sweetness, a capacity to dream and gain joy from every facet of existence. If the Warrior is the master of war, she is the artist of peace. The Warrior saves her from the Dragon, but she is the one who brings happiness to the Warrior's life, because the Warrior knows how to fight but she knows how to live. Contrary to popular perceptions, Warrior and Princess are not separate entities, but energies that complement each other. Balance in a person, man or woman that he or she may be, is achieved when there is harmony between these opposites.

One of humanity's tragedies is that most people have lost (or just never had) the capacity to be warriors and princesses, and settled for being the shadows of what they could be. One of martial arts' tragedies is that although most martial artists remember the Warrior's spirit, they have lost the Princess along the way. In the majority of cases, the air within martial arts schools is soaked with testosterone. Often, a climate of cocky machismo dominates the place. It is not simply a result of the fact that most martial artists are men. What is lacking is not only the presence of women, but the presence of a balance between so-called "masculine" and "feminine" qualities. Too much yang, too little yin. The display of toughness, hard muscles, and barbaric screams takes center stage, whereas the development of a balanced personality is forgotten in the locker room. The roughest aspects of the Warrior figure are those to which most attention is paid. The ability to defeat an opponent in as little time as possible, the victory in tournaments, and the building of a monumental ego are the goals of many practitioners. However, if these goals (which to a degree can be legitimate) are the only goals, then there is little difference between a street-fighting bully and a martial artist. Philosophy, art, gentleness and spirituality should be the focus of a martial artist's attention not less than technical proficiency in combat. Unlike a simple street-fighter, who only knows how to beat the hell out of someone, a martial artist should be the living synthesis of warrior power and feminine sensitivity.

Since time immemorial, women have often relied on weapons other than physical strength. In addition to the fact that men are naturally endowed with more muscular strength than women, many religions and cultural conventions have conspired to cast a very negative judgment on any woman who tried to develop "masculine" qualities such as strength and fighting ability. Women, defenseless and weak, were supposed to stay in the corner, look pretty and depend on the help of the physically superior males. Praise to a little boy who play-wrestles with his friends, but shame on a little girl who does the same. By restricting women's access to the training tools of physical self-empowerment, this type of cultural conditioning exacerbated further the natural differences between men and women, and relegated women to a subordinate position. The world of physical strength was to be—as James Brown sang—"a Man's World." The fact that this lack of familiarity with their physical strength also affected women's independence, emotional ability to stand on their own, and self-esteem was a more or less intentional by-product of the teachings of religions and philosophies that had little patience for strong, assertive women.

Let's think of the Judeo-Christian tradition, for example, in which women originate from a lonely guy's rib in order to provide him with some entertainment and relieve him of his boredom. In such a tradition, obviously, strength and assertiveness are not only useless qualities for a woman, but they are downright contrary to the very purpose for which women came into being. Becoming independent and self-confident is hardly fitting for a being whose sole purpose is to amuse a man and be ready to follow his commands.

The practice of martial arts can offer women some very revolutionary tools to counter the conditioning of this type of cultural traditions. Thanks to martial arts, women have the occasion to come in contact with their long-repressed yang energy and physical power without having to turn into androgynous-looking, steroid-fed machines. Becoming able to trust one's ability to defend oneself and fight, and taking on a role other than that of prey or victim, pushes fear away. When you know that you can flatten to the ground stronger, bigger men, something inside can afford to relax, for the moment in which you know the real measure of your power, you don't have to put on a show to prove your worth. If you know how to fight, peace is a choice. In this way, a woman can stop seeing herself as weak and defenseless in both body and character.

The martial arts, like perhaps nothing else in the world, teach the way of being warriors, because martial arts are the perfect physical medium that allows us to embody the theoretical principles of the way of the warrior. Any self-respecting living being needs to also be a warrior. Pushing it to the limit, I would say that it is very hard to enjoy a full life without becoming warriors.

Of course, I'm not inviting sweet ladies and innocent children to turn into bloodthirsty barbarians ready to butcher the neighbors. Becoming warriors doesn't mean that we have to learn how to beat up others. The warrior's way doesn't necessarily pass through the practice of the martial arts. Many people who have never seen or even heard of a dojo and who have never fought other than in battles of Dungeons & Dragons, have nonetheless applied in practice the way of the warrior, sometimes without even being aware of it. My father, for example, used to consider my passion for martial arts with the same enthusiasm that a vegetarian displays at the prospect of a field trip to the slaughterhouse. However, he has taught me more about applying a warrior's attitude to daily life than any martial artist has ever done.

The essential attribute of the Warrior is the refusal to give away one's power. Family, friends, schoolteachers, political parties, churches, gangs ... the catalogue of volunteers willing to influence our decisions is longer than I can list. However, regardless of good intentions, no form of conditioning can help us: neither the dogmas of political and religious authorities nor the emotional pressures of those who are close to us. For this reason, the Warrior is essential. Becoming strong enough to prevent anything and anyone from bossing us around, both physically and emotionally, is what allows us to be truly free. Without this, we can be crushed by external pressures at any moment.

The soldier, like any other agent at the service of totalitarian powers, is the antithesis of the Warrior's spirit. The Warrior eats up an army for breakfast because the Warrior is an individual, whereas the army is made up of numbers and "yes sir" whose character and individuality are repressed by the necessity to subordinate to the military machine. The Warrior doesn't go to die in a war he doesn't believe in. Whereas the essence of a good soldier is obeying and following orders without thinking, the nature of a Warrior is to choose even when only one choice seems available. The Warrior is his own boss. He is an individualist in the best sense of the word. He follows the advice of anyone who can convince him and gives heart and soul to those who touch his heart, but no one can give him orders or force him to act against his will. The Warrior is an iconoclast who refuses to put his fate in the hands of any superior authority.

Responsibility is a word that many bad habits have twisted around. It reminds me of some sadistic schoolteachers' mantra.

Normally, anyone who doesn't sell their soul to the slavery of an economically secure but emotionally stifling job is accused of irresponsibility. Lies. Huge lies. Being responsible doesn't mean sacrificing our freedom on the altar of Duty. It means doing anything to make our lives worthy of our dreams. The quintessence of the Warrior is in swearing loyalty to one's own visions.

Once, when I was fourteen, as I was being boiled by the sun on a deserted beach, I was touched by the simplest, most direct and most revolutionary revelation that I could imagine: we are the ones creating our surroundings. Everything that we can see and touch is there because we accept it to be so. Our houses, the state of our physical bodies, our friends, our jobs are all the results of our choices. Once we remember this, it becomes possible to turn into artists of living.

Every day, everywhere we turn, we are told that if we want to be successful we should quit chasing utopian ideals and should instead settle for more modest goals. We hear this message so many times that we end up believing it, and we begin setting limits on our range of possibilities. Resignation becomes our God. We take every instance in which things don't turn out the way we want them and use it as an irrefutable proof of the fact that life is hard and can't be changed much. If we could only find enough confidence to quit worshipping our self-imposed limits, we might be able to transform our lives and become the people we want to be. There is no prize at the end of an unhappy life. Reality often blocks our way with traps and obstacles and that's why we need the Warrior.

The warrior myth is not destined only for those interested in combat, but is for all living beings. Everyone experiences the conflict between reality and their desires. Those who lack a Warrior's attitude are left powerless after the first few defeats. Without the Warrior, we are in the hands of fate. Our choices have no power. Whereas many people are content with surviving, the warrior carves for himself a chance to choose his destiny. He doesn't wait in the hope that things may happen, but makes them happen. Of course, it can be scary to think that everything depends on our choices. It is much easier to pass the responsibility onto somebody else. There is something reassuring in delegating to others our power of choice and then being able to blame them if things go wrong. If we don't feel up to the task, complaining is always easier than creating.

This, however, is the coward's way, not the Warrior's. The Warrior doesn't complain nor he blames others for every problem. The Warrior takes all the responsibility on himself. He doesn't look for alibis for his failures. In the game of basketball, for example, there are moments when good players fade into the background and warriors emerge. When with ten seconds left on the clock the game is still on the line, the Warrior wants the ball in his hands. When all the pressure is on you and fear is screaming in your ears, that's when it is possible to see warrior spirits in action. Michael Jordan, Kobe Bryant and Mike D'Antoni (the best player to ever grace the game of basketball in Italy) come to my mind. Even if up until that point they have played a bad game, they are tired and the defenders are breathing down their necks, they want the ball. It would be easy to let someone else take all the pressure and responsibility but, if defeat has to come, warriors prefer to go down by their own doing. Jordan, Kobe, or D'Antoni can make mistakes like any other human being, but the difference is that they don't ever stop irradiating a feeling of complete confidence. This is why, when the tough times arrive, they have the courage and determination to take and often make the deciding shot.

Being afraid is normal. Everyone is afraid of messing up and having to pay the consequences. Often we hide our fears because we feel unable to face them, but this is how fear begins working us on the inside, conditioning our behavior without our conscious knowledge. Fear imposes limits that don't belong to us. The Warrior is not afraid of being afraid. He accepts it, looks it in the eyes, and challenges it. Refusing to be a hostage in the hands of one's fears is the act of a Warrior.

From everything written so far, it should be clear that I don't underestimate the development of warrior qualities. But then what? If the Warrior was left to himself, life would be a battlefield. Nietzsche writes "Free *from* what? As if that mattered.... But your eyes should tell me brightly: free *for* what?" Once we have cultivated the warrior's willpower and strength of character, but still ignore gentleness, softness, and love, what have we gained? Maybe we can free ourselves from all the external tyrants, but if we are our own tyrants, we are still in chains. If the warrior's strength doesn't go hand in hand with the Princess' grace and sweetness, the warrior is not much more than an efficient killer (if the Warrior metaphor is taken literally) or a simple problem-solver (if the Warrior image is taken in its widest sense.) In either case, he may be a god at fighting trouble, but unable to give life. He conquers freedom but doesn't know how to use it. This is the reason why political revolutions inevitably fail. After taking down the dictatorship oppressing them, revolutionaries often lose the purpose of their existence. Once they have the power to decide how to run their own lives, they don't know what to do anymore. As long as there was a tyrant to be killed, everybody agreed and life was relatively simple. But when the tyrant is dead and it's no longer time anymore to complain or to fight but to create, big troubles begin. War is easy. Peace is much more complicated. Too busy fighting in order to cultivate their hearts and love for life, many revolutionaries turn themselves into oppressors because they never received the Princess' kiss, nor have they learned from her how to live in beauty. Hindu mythology tells that, when he is alone, Shiva can only destroy. His power in battle is extraordinary, and there is no enemy, man or god, who can stand up to him. He can take down armies and conquer kingdoms, but he also can't create anything. Only when he enjoys the favor of the goddess, can Shiva create. It is her feminine energy that makes Shiva able to give life. Without her, Shiva is like a Warrior who hasn't freed the Princess.

A Warrior who doesn't know softness is far from being complete as much as a Princess who doesn't know strength. Not everyone can be sensitive, poetic, and kind, but if we don't also know how to be warriors, any shallow bully can walk all over our kindness and poetic sensitivity. The Princess has a winged heart, a priceless imagination, and the ability to make everyday life magical, but as soon as an obstacle blocks her way she is stuck, completely unable to overcome it. She knows how to dream, but doesn't know how to walk in the world. Since she is not able to defend her own space, she becomes an easy prey for the Dragon. She is never free to choose without the fear that something beyond her control may frustrate her desires. Fear follows her step after step. It is the same fear experienced by smaller animals who know that if they stumble upon a predator they have no way to face him. It is not just a matter of muscles, but of attitude. The fear is not only the fear of a physical confrontation. It runs much deeper. It is the anxiety that comes from lack of self-confidence, from not trusting one's capacity to face trouble. Often, people with amazing creative abilities and with uncommon sensitivity suffer more than most because their talents may not produce concrete results in the world and they lack the Warrior's strength to fight until they overcome all obstacles. But when inside someone's heart the creative tenderness of the Princess lives in company with the Warrior's character, normal limitations lose their power and an individual is free to move the first step on life's dancing floor. The union between feminine and masculine is the union between will and power.

The Princess is the heart's messenger. She doesn't need a magnifying glass to see the difference between real life and a plastic imitation. She reminds us that we are not part of a TV set or of an office's furniture. She makes us dream and tremble with passion, showing us that living in beauty is our right and duty, and that settling for anything less than happiness is the blueprint for mediocrity. The Princess' creativity smuggles for us images stolen from life lived in the best of possible worlds. Putting his strength to the service of his dreams, the Warrior helps turn these visions into reality. With a roar, he removes all obstacles in order to open for us a path to making our lives a masterpiece created by a happy god.

Some of the most mythical warriors populating the Olympus of martial arts have become famous not simply for their legendary feats as fighters, but also for the serenity of their spirits. The descriptions we have of them often coincide. Calm, relaxed, peaceful men with a genuine love for life. They walked along the Warrior's path because it takes an indomitable spirit to be able to live beyond conflict, but once they have reached their goals, the fighter's intensity was put to rest in order to make room for gentleness. As Nietzsche put it, "I have become one who blesses and says Yes; and I fought long for that and was a fighter that I might one day get my hands free to bless."

They keep the Warrior's power handy in case of need, but they lack the rigidity of those who never remove their armor. Morihei Ueshiba, the founder of Aikido, is perhaps a perfect example. As he himself declared, "The way of the warrior is the creation of harmony." Within him feminine and masculine were united in a way that granted him unlimited access to happiness' kingdom. The Princess had drawn a smile on the Warrior's face. Throughout the centuries, many other martial artists, like Ueshiba, have been not just fighters, but also poets, healers, painters, artists: individuals full of joy and warmth, inspired by a deep sense of love for life. There is no contradiction between having a Warrior's power and tender feelings. The heart of a Warrior is not made to be fenced with barbed wire. His heart is sweet. This is the main reason to become warriors in the first place: in order to be strong enough to turn our sensitivity into a source of joy rather than of suffering.

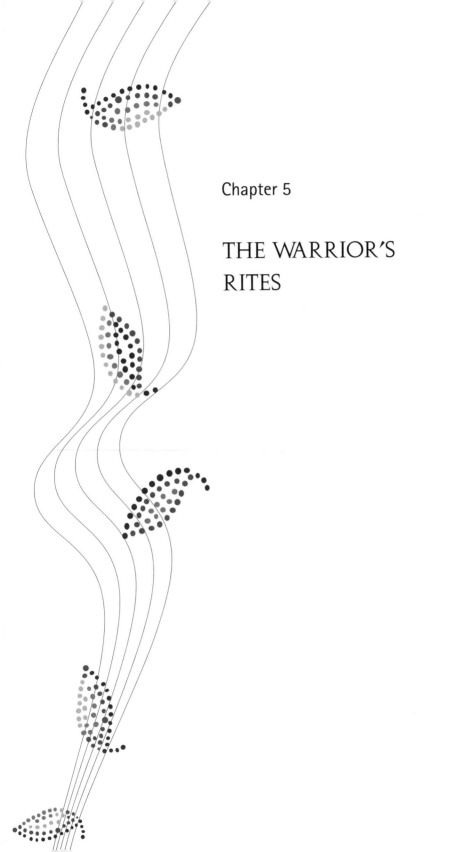

Chapter 5

THE WARRIOR'S RITES

IN THE DOJO

There are places where linear time doesn't enjoy any authority whatsoever. Places where worries and mental troubles can be left at the door, and where the voice of a deeper awareness whispers in the ears of our soul. Sacred spaces where we go to find ourselves and from which we walk away changed and restored.

Some American Indian peoples say that the sweat lodge is the womb of the earth. Those who enter immerse themselves in a cleansing bath that washes away the dust of daily life. When people emerge from the darkness and the heat of the lodge, they see the world with new eyes, with the innocence of someone who has just been reborn.

A sweat lodge, a cathedral, a sacred mountain, a temple, an oracle, or a martial arts dojo ... in these places, a magic essence pervades the air, as if the laws that normally govern us were lifted and everything became possible. It is here—far away from social conventions, from the haste of a rhythm that doesn't truly belong to us, from other peoples' opinions, from the problems we believe to have—it is in these places beyond Time that our true nature speaks to us and teaches us how to live.

Translated more or less literally from Japanese, the dojo is "the place where to find the way" or, if we set free our poetic license, "the place of enlightenment." From these words, it is easy to guess that to martial artists the dojo represents something more than just a physical building in which to practice. It is a ceremonial center for facing one's weaknesses and for cultivating the seeds of one's power. The intensity of the training doesn't permit us to take inside the dojo the problems of everyday life, and requires such total concentration that no room is left for our consciousness to get distracted chasing the thread of thoughts. Entering the dojo is like entering another dimension where our social identity is nothing but a useless obstacle.

Just like an individual taking part in a sweat lodge stops before the entrance to get purified in the smoke of burning sage, the martial artist, before crossing the invisible line that separates the dojo from the rest of the world, stops at the door and salutes in the traditional way (either bowing or placing the right fist against the left palm, depending on the tradition), thus signaling the transition from the normal state of consciousness to the ceremonial space. Once the border is crossed, the rite begins. The martial artist takes off the clothes he or she wears in daily life and puts on a ceremonial costume fit for the occasion: a Judo gi, a *Kendo* armor, or maybe one of the silk uniforms of Northern Chinese martial arts. Whatever the choice may be the psychological effect is the same. Just like football players before the game or fighters before going into battle paint their faces with war colors, the martial artist gives his consciousness the signal that it is time to tune into a different frequency. To emphasize this shift of consciousness, at the beginning of the lesson, the master of a dojo where I trained for a short time, would close the entrance by drawing a huge curtain and would tell the students to leave society outside.

In the course of a couple of hours of martial arts practice, we encounter such a vast number of symbols and ritual actions as to make any anthropologist happy for a lifetime. The dojo is one of those few non-religious places in our society where adults can give themselves permission to come directly in contact with Myth. In a dojo, an individual can experience principles and ideals through his muscles, and can come to touch the warrior archetype in a socially acceptable way.

WHEN I REMEMBER WHO I AM, NOTHING IS A PROBLEM: THE PRACTICE

When the sun scorches the earth as it shines in all its might and drought drains the energies of every waterway, Polynesian shamans set themselves on the path. For many miles they walk upstream along the dry bed of the river until they reach the source. There they sit down, bend toward the dehydrated ear of the spring and begin telling the river the story of its birth. Listening to the story, the river remembers its nature. As soon as the shaman takes the first steps on his way back, he can already hear the voice of the running water.

Actually, no Polynesian shaman ever behaved in this manner except in my father's imagination. He wrote this story many years ago. If I remember well, it was very short, just a few lines longer than the synopsis I just gave, but it struck me deeply. It wasn't because it was very different from anything else he had ever written, but also because, as I read it, I felt as though it put a finger on a question of vital importance. The shaman only needs to remind the river of its nature and then, there is no drought that can keep it from flowing. The same thing happens to people. No master and no method can give us something that we don't already possess. The only thing that can help us is a stimulus to remind us of who we truly are.

Western philosophy would say that this is the old Socratic idea of knowledge as memory, but in this case Socrates didn't invent anything that shamanic cultures didn't already know. For thousands of years, our ancestors have given life to rituals whose main function is to bring us back in contact with our spirits and "remember" ourselves. No river always flows without stopping and no individual is always fully present one hundred percent. Highs and lows are natural parts of experience that cannot be avoided. But what really matters is knowing how to quickly find the stimuli to get back in tune with our vital potential. As Aikido founder Morihei Ueshiba said; "I lose my balance all the time but I regain it so fast that you don't see me lose it at all."

The practice of martial arts is a ritual that helps me to remember who I am. Remembering who I am is the only thing I really need, but it is a never-ending task, because forgetting is very easy and equally easy is not realizing I have forgotten. Maybe our ideas, words and opinions remain the same, but inside a light fades. We still are who we are, but just a little less intense, less passionate, less alive, less of the person we can be. When this happens, what we need is to go through an experience that turns the switch back on. Going to practice in a dojo three or four times a week can be one of these experiences.

I am sure that potentially anything can be a stimulus, but I don't like being in the hands of fate. This is why I am naturally attracted by the consistency of a discipline like martial arts. Aah! I have written in the same sentence two words for which my father could disown me, especially considering that I got here starting from a story he wrote. "Consistency" and "discipline" are ugly words. They sound like the battle-cry of a team of Bulgarian Stakhanovite laborers. It is true that at times language forgets to court the Muse of poetry, but in this case it is better to avoid being too squeamish. I call for Chogyam Trungpa's help: "By discipline we do not mean something unpleasant or artificial that is imposed from outside. Rather, this discipline is an organic process that expands naturally from our own experience.... For him [the warrior], discipline is not a demand but a pleasure." And Deng Ming Dao adds: "Discipline is freedom, and the companion to imagination. Discipline makes it possible for you to become whatever you want to be."

Regular practice of a discipline like martial arts can be compared to sweeping the floor. It is not something we can do once, achieve a result and forget about it. Every day dust comes back and soon will cover the floor again. Only regular practice can keep the dust away. Contrary to those experiences that burn with intensity but only take place occasionally, the power of martial arts is found in repetition. When we begin enjoying our training, consistency is not a boring duty to be done in order to obtain a distant goal. Training is a pleasure onto itself. Spending two hours in the ceremonial space of the dojo is something to look forward to. Even the physical effectiveness of martial arts depends on consistency. Certain movements, repeated hundreds of times, become part of our natural reflexes to the point that they can be executed completely by instinct, without the interference of any rational thought. The body remembers even when the mind is clouded.

THE MASTER

In order to be respected, authority has got to be respectable.

—Tom Robbins

Inside the dojo, the master is the head of the house, the conductor of the symphony, the undisputed leader. He has the last word on anything that happens in the dojo, but he also has a huge responsibility: he is the channel through which the beauty and the effectiveness of centuries-old traditions pass. If he doesn't teach well, the students will learn poor techniques and bad attitudes, and in turn they will pass these mistakes to future generations. On his character and on his ability rests the destiny of the art he represents. A master makes too many mistakes and the art becomes watered-down and soon is lost: a great weight on the shoulders of one individual alone.

For many years, the great importance placed on the figure of the master kept me away from martial arts. I had already abandoned basketball because I was allergic to my coaches' attitudes. Anytime one of them raised his voice to yell at me or tried to give me orders that I didn't approve of, I took extreme care to let them know where they could stick their orders, and then I continued playing in my own way. (All the power to Dennis Rodman!) As far as I can remember, I have always been naturally restive in the face of any form of authority. I have never been able to look with respect into the eyes of those who subordinate their own individuality in order to obey a master and follow blindly his or her method. Most of the time, those looking with admiring eyes at "The Master" and praising his virtues are people with very little self-esteem. My first impulse when I meet those revered as masters is to challenge them and pull them down from the pedestal.

With these premises, it is needless to say that I was less than enthusiastic at the idea of studying a discipline in which the master has such a primary role. In martial arts, in fact, the quality of the master is almost more important than the art itself. In the hands of the wrong teacher, even the deepest internal art can become empty and crude, and vice versa a skilled master can turn a technically rough art into poetry in motion.

I had loved martial arts even before starting to practice them, but too many times I had heard of teachers treating their students with maximum severity but no respect. For years, I continued searching for a teacher who could be compatible with my character. Soon after the beginning of my search, one thing became immediately clear. It is much easier to be a great martial artist than a good teacher. I met people with extraordinary physical abilities, people who had themselves called by all kinds of honorific titles (Sensei, Sifu, Masters, Grandmasters and even Great-grandmasters), but in the midst of this crowd of great names, very few were the teachers who deserved to be considered as such. Even if they were not the authoritarian neo-nazis I hated, some only had a superficial knowledge of the art, others were true experts but had no clue regarding how to teach what they themselves knew, and still others lacked the patience, the gentleness and the charisma of a true leader. William Blake kept coming to mind: "The eagle never lost so much time as when he submitted to learn of the crow."

Then, one day, the moment I stepped in the door of a dojo, I knew that I had found what I was looking for. For four years, I had visited hundreds of schools and met with many famous masters, but I had never had such a clear feeling. Only about ten students were training under the guidance of a smiling giant. I had never seen such a big man moving with that kind of agility. Grace and power were obvious in his every gesture. Upon second look, I noticed that the man was not quite so huge, just about six-foot-two and 210 pounds, but his intensity made him appear much bigger than he was. He was there one hundred percent. His presence filled the entire room. He didn't require his students to bow or to call him master. Instead, he had everyone call him by name and treated his students as friends: exactly the kind of teacher I had been looking for, someone I could really respect. This wasn't the respect that comes from an artificial discipline, from a coercive authority, or from his great fame. What inspired the deepest respect was the man, his personality, his example.

Less than a year after I began training with him, my teacher got married and decided to retire. And I was left having to again look for a new instructor. But at this point I was hooked. The art fascinated me to a point that I simply couldn't stop practicing no matter what. Also, my search didn't take long because in that year I had learned one thing. Chasing a romantic illusion of what a master is supposed to be like is not healthy. No teacher can compare to an idealized all-wise, all-powerful, compassionate yet demanding, archetype. The master is nothing but a guide offering his students the gift of physical technique, and for lack of an ideal teacher, it is up to the students to become their own masters.

THE WEAPONS

> *At the moment of shooting the arrow, one's true nature is discovered.*
>
> —Zen Saying

Physical objects are inorganic matter without personality or vital energy. They don't breathe. They don't speak. They don't have a beating heart. They don't have character or emotions. Considering physical objects as something inert and inanimate is popular wisdom in Western culture.

But what does Western popular wisdom know about the power of objects? Has it ever heard the voice of a shamanic drum speaking? Has it ever seen an Indian medicine man praying with the pipe to the four directions? Has it ever spent the night in the forge of a Japanese blacksmith watching, in the midst of flashes of fire, the birth of a traditional sword? There are objects that are not simple tools and are more than works of art. Objects created from the same material legends are made of. Holding them in one's hands, you can feel their power flowing in your fingers. "Inert" is the last word that comes to mind to describe them. I have seen objects that were much more alive than many people.

The particular energy vibrating in some objects didn't escape the attention of the warriors of the past. If to some Indian tribes, the pipe is the traditional altar through which they can communicate with the universe, a warrior's weapons are his most trusted companions, the physical extensions of his character. The sword, the spear, the staff, a pair of butterfly knives, the *Kali* sticks, the bow and the arrows; every one of these weapons is made with different materials and has a particular shape, usage and history. But what matters most are the different spiritual qualities of each weapon. Each one has an energy that is different from all the others. Depending on which weapon a warrior decides to seize, he can come in contact with different forces. It is something you can feel as soon as you hold them up. Archery invites a mix of inner peace and total focus. The staff is the weapon of those who don't want any bloodshed, the weapon of traveling monks: strong but not overtly violent. On the contrary, training with Kali sticks draws me into a mental state of rare harshness that doesn't offer or ask for pity, and isn't satisfied until it sees tangible signs of destruction.

Not only do different kinds of weapons evoke different types of energy, but every individual weapon is charged with its very own power: in the whole world no two swords are exactly alike. For this reason, a very strong bond ties a warrior to his favorite weapon. They become inseparable, as if they shared the same vital force. The sword, for example, is the soul of the samurai. It represents his way of life and his code of honor. It is the embodiment of *Bushido*. The same is true of King Arthur and his sword. By drawing the sword from the rock, Arthur became king: Excalibur is at the same time the living symbol of the ideal of chivalry and the heart of the kingdom of Camelot.

Since such weapons are made of more than just raw matter, giving birth to a weapon is not only a work of art and technology, but is also a religious ritual. Before forging a sword, Japanese blacksmiths purify themselves, the forge and all the working tools. At times, among some American Indian tribes, in order to make a shield, a warrior would invite his friends to help him and together they would pray to bestow power upon the object. Then, the shield would be decorated according to the vision of its future carrier. Once the work was over, a medicine man would come to bless it.

A man creating a weapon with his own hands can charge it with his energy. All the hours in which the creator devotes religious attention to the work at hand fill the piece with a kind of energy that is unknown in mass-produced objects. For this reason, in the best of all possible worlds, a martial artist should create with his own hands at least one of the weapons that he uses. It is a touching experience that radically transforms the way of looking at the material world. Once I worked on a long bamboo, shaping it into a fighting staff. There is no comparison between the feeling I have when I hold this staff and what I feel when I hold any other kind of weapon which may be technically superior but also very impersonal.

The use of traditional weapons is an essential part of martial arts practice. Almost any style of martial arts includes the study of some weapons in its syllabus, and there are even arts such as *Kyudo*, the way of archery, and Kendo, the way of the sword, which are completely dedicated to the study of a single weapon. In ancient times, the practice with the weapons was aimed at maximum effectiveness, because the survival of the warrior depended on it. But in modern times, when it is obviously anachronistic to walk around with a samurai sword attached to one's waist or to think of having to defend oneself against an aggressor charging with a spear, the study of weapons has a value that goes beyond self-defense. Learning how to use one of the traditional weapons as if it were a natural extension of their arms teaches martial artists a deeper perception of space and distance. Or rather, the work with weapons can become a moving meditation of incredible beauty: like a Zen koan in which if you don't pay enough attention to the weapon you will hit yourself, but if you worry too much about it you will be lacking power, grace and fluidity. Practicing with a real blade, even within the walls of a controlled environment like the dojo, and with many safety precautions, instills a monastic concentration even in the most distracted martial artist.

But today, maybe the main function of traditional weapons is mythological. Learning how to use them, we come in contact with the historical past of the martial arts and with the power of myths. It is true that—as Dumbo teaches—the power to fly doesn't lie in the magic feather. It is within us. And it is also true than worshipping an object more than the person holding it is the beginning of fetishism, but weapons are symbolic reminders of the spirit of the warrior's way.

KATA AND FORMS

It takes two people to have a fight, but what happens when a lone martial artist wants to challenge himself? For lack of opponents made of flesh and blood, imaginary fighters can be invited to play along. Forms (Katas in Japanese martial arts) are codified sequences of movements and fighting techniques that the martial artist practices alone, cutting the air with strikes aimed at invisible enemies. The English language has an evocative formula that can be used to describe forms: "shadow boxing." Practicing forms is something common to nearly all styles of martial arts. Every art has its own. Whether it is the acrobatic wonders of *Wushu* forms, the raw power of Karate katas, or the slow smoothness of Tai Chi Chuan forms, the essence doesn't change. Every form contains the fundamental principles and the core of the art.

Watching a master executing a form, it becomes easy to understand why martial arts are called "arts." Even an untrained eye can see the fluid beauty of a form. It is like a fighting dance. To be fascinated, the people watching don't have to be martial artists nor do they need to understand the application of each movement. But the seemingly effortless execution of a form is the result of many, many hours of practice. Remembering all the movements is but the first step of training in forms. Then, the real work begins. The attention paid to every tiny detail is what makes the difference.

Just as a Zen parable, at the beginning the martial artist acts by instinct, without being fully aware of what he or she is doing, so the result is a shallow form without flavor, rhythm or intensity. In the words of Chinese masters "it doesn't have kung fu." Then, after training for a long time to make every technique precise, the martial artist is aware of every gesture and knows all the subtle secrets that make the form a pleasure to watch. His form is now quick, powerful, spectacular. The rhythm is captivating, the movements perfect, and onlookers clap with enthusiasm seeing how hard the martial artist has worked to reach this goal. But something is still missing. It still doesn't have true kung fu. Still too much thinking and worrying about doing everything right. The martial artist is heavy under the weight of his knowledge. Too present in the form is the memory of the hardship of the training. Too much sweat, too much effort. At this point, he is an expert, has learned everything needed: now it is time to start forgetting, or rather, to remember without remembering. As Lao Tzu writes: "In comprehending all knowledge, can you renounce the mind?" Again, just as when he knew nothing about the form, the martial artist goes back to acting by instinct. Not the rough instinct of those who have never learned, but the instinct of those who, after learning, have gone beyond it. Natural, light movements, precise down to the millimeter without betraying any shadow of effort: a concentrate of power and grace. Finally, he "has kung fu." Now, the form has spirit.

To execute a perfect form, the martial artist forgets every other thing and tunes in to the energy of the form. It is like emptying one's mind in order to interpret a role. In certain Chinese martial arts, the names of the movements don't simply describe the gestures. They are oracular messages suggesting to the martial artist which type of energy has to be called forth. Poetic flashes to be meditated upon before practice. Names like "the black dragon turns its tail," "the hero chops down a mountain," "the squirrels exit their nests," "forgive me if I do not follow you," "picking a needle at the bottom of the sea," "the child worships the Buddha," "the fierce tiger descends the mountain," "the hero gives a party."

Few things teach how to be focused here and now like forms

do. Forms are like solitary rituals dedicated to the achievement of physical as well as spiritual perfection. When the form is alive, awareness, body and mind become one. The eyes glow like fires. When you feel this sensation, you know that the form will be perfect, even before moving a single finger.

STYLES (PART I)

Maybe I have spent too much time reading fairy tales. I was taught that martial arts are a physical and philosophical practice aimed at making us better people. But reading many books and magazines, you get the impression that many martial artists spend more time quarreling among themselves than they do refining their characters. Division rules, and the meaning of Budo is lost in personal rivalries, power struggles, associations fighting with each other for the title of being the only true one representing a certain art. Accusing each other of incompetence, trying to ruin others' reputations, and declaring that any style, with the exception of one's own, is ineffective and useless, are very common practices among martial artists. The habit is so popular that escaping this kind of controversy is far from easy. Even first-class martial artists, even people who are otherwise sensitive and intelligent, let themselves be carried away in these verbal fights.

Unfortunately, however, this disease is not limited to martial arts. It is something common to different ages and geographical spaces, deeply engrained in the most diverse types of experience. It almost seems that the more an experience possesses life and beauty, the more it is likely to attract dogmas, contradictions and conflicts and to be always in danger of producing effects which are opposite to the spirit with which it was born. Among American Indians I have seen exceptional individuals spending their time fueling petty jealousy and harshly criticizing each other: medicine men caught up in local feuds, Sun Dancers praying with body and soul during the day and engaging in rivalries, gossip and name-calling in the evening. People who could have the energy to change the world getting lost in divisions and sectarianism. It is sad and pathetic to see so much talent being wasted.

American Indian religion, like martial arts, like Chinese traditional medicine, or like any other field of experience we feel like adding to the list; poisoning one's character arguing rather than creating. Different martial art styles follow the example that has been set by different religions for hundreds of years. The members of nearly every religion, just like practitioners of nearly every martial art style, argue that they are the only ones having the Way, the Method, the exclusive telephone line to God's office. The followers of different religions, just like the followers of different martial arts, consider those who choose a different path as the "heathens." In the name of ideology, rival fronts and factions are born. This is the result of the mix of dogma and egocentrism. An aggressive fanaticism that can't tolerate those choices that are not contemplated by one's system of thought. Often, the discourses of martial artist are soaked with a similar self-righteous intolerance.

But, luckily, there are just as many martial artists who don't have any inclination to this kind of "Holy War" mentality. Individuals who have no intention to reduce the breadth of their visions to a fight between rival gangs and who don't wish to turn martial arts into a battlefield between "us" and "them." The love for the art they practice doesn't blind them to the beauty of other styles. Every art has a particular energy that no other style has. The different kinds of martial arts are nothing but paths to reach the summit of the mountain. Stopping along the way to speculate about which path is the best is a distraction leading us away from our destination.

A Buddhist monk once said; "If you meet the Buddha, kill him." Inspired by a similar iconoclast passion, Bruce Lee rejected the dogmatism that often surrounds some traditional schools, and created his own style of martial arts. Like the Zen monk, Lee understood that blindly following an established method is not the best way to develop one's own potentials. After a method gives you everything it has to offer, it is useless to remain attached to it. Following Buddha, one doesn't become a Buddha. However, Bruce Lee's visionary and anarchic syncretism is not antithetical to the traditional styles any more than Zen is antithetical to Buddhism. Zen philosophy and Bruce Lee just shake tradition when it loses its spirit and becomes dogmatic. Syncretism and tradition are the opposite faces of the Tao that bring balance to one another.

STYLES (PART II)

The title of today's lesson is "Syncretism and Information-Exchange as Paradigms of Knowledge in the Age of Globalization." Leading the panel, we have Professors Frank Shamrock, Maurice Smith, and Tsuyoshi Kohsaka. Contrary to what you may imagine, I'm not inviting you to step into a dusty university hall to listen to a lecture held by equally dusty scholars whose brains have become too heavy due to the accumulation of useless information and lack of sunshine. No, the theater of today's lesson is an octagon surrounded by an iron cage, where some of the best martial artists on the planet challenge each other in a competition made with few rules and much adrenaline. Welcome to the world of multicultural beatings where knowledge is not a theory or something to be debated, but is sweat, technique, muscles, and heart.

When in the early 1990s, the two main North American organizations of Mixed Martial Arts, Ultimate Fighting Championship (UFC) and Extreme Fighting (EF), invited martial artists to quit boasting about their skills and come test their ideas in a competition open to everyone, the experts of most every kind of martial art jumped into the ring to defend the honor of their style. "Which martial arts style will come out on top?" was the question on everyone's lips.

Now that, after years of competition, the answer is clear, shock and disbelief rule. No style comes out on top. The experts of particular styles, in fact, routinely meet a miserable end on the sacrificial altar of global knowledge. Regularly, the specialists who dedicate their lives to the study of a single kind of art are swept away by the warriors of synthesis, the martial artists who take the best from several styles and combine it all in a personal mix. Bruce Lee, who already thirty years ago prophesied that the devotion to a single style was a disease, is probably somewhere with a big smile on his face.

Among all the UFC and EF fighters, no one can tell this story better than Shamrock, Smith, and Kohsaka. In fact, it is hard to find an example of the dominion of syncretism in the age of globalization better than the one provided by their alliance. Before meeting each other, the three were already known for their incredible martial talents. The African-American Maurice Smith had already been a champion in Thai Boxing and Extreme Fighting. The Japanese Kohsaka was a fourth degree black belt in Judo with several years of victories on his record. And after only six months of training in submission fighting, Frank Juarez Shamrock, a young man of Native American and Mexican heritage who had been adopted by an Irish family, had begun to conquer the world of martial arts by demolishing any opponent who stepped in his way. Not satisfied, the three decided to combine their talents and learn from each other. The result was beyond anyone's expectations. Smith became the Ultimate Fighting heavy weight champion thanks to the ground-fighting techniques taught by Kohsaka and Shamrock. Thanks to Smith's teachings, on the other hand, Kohsaka arrived just a step away from the title, while Shamrock retired as the undefeated middle weight champion. Those still believing that specialists have a future should go test their theories with the alliance of professors of martial syncretism.

Chapter 6

MARTIAL ARTS, MEDIA, AND MYTH

Five minutes of painfully bad acting lead us to what we have been waiting for. Barbaric screams, flying kicks, and bodies being thrown across the room. Since all good things are doomed to end eventually, this scene gives way to another sad attempt at following the long-lost cousin of a decent script. Don't worry, though. The limping dialogue will soon stop, and again we will be treated to a scene of the wounded but victorious hero getting rid of twelve ugly, evil guys thanks to his martial ability. Following the uncertain steps of a poorly patched together plot made of revenge and deadly tournaments, the film will continue alternating a few minutes of acting and a few minutes of flashy fights until the credits start rolling. Welcome to the wonderful world of martial arts movies.

Let's move on to video games. As an appetizer, we can start with *Shaq-Fu,* a game about basketball champion Shaquille O'Neal who gets caught in an interplanetary martial arts tournament, and is forced to rely on his art of Shaq-ki-do to fight a martial circus of voodoo witches and alien monsters. Moving on to the main dish, here is *Mortal Kombat,* where parallel universes come together for a tournament populated by ninjas, amazons, warlords and mutant freaks, and where the highlights are the graphic decapitations of the defeated enemies.

In case decapitations are not your thing, let's turn to the good old printed words of journalism. Macho posturing and mean expressions, which supposedly are to demonstrate how manly and tough are the fighters sporting them, dominate the covers of most martial arts magazines. The contents of the magazines are often a little more promising. Here and there it is definitely possible to find useful information. However, in order to get to it, one has to dig through articles about rival federations competing for the title of the only legitimate organization representing a particular style, or about "masters" spending the best part of their energies trashing each others' reputation, or yet about self-proclaimed killing machines boasting of their bone-crushing skills.

Is it just my impression or could the public image of martial arts use some improvement? It seems that mainly the flashiest, most violent aspects of martial arts that catch the spotlight in the media. Of the day-to-day reality of martial arts practice hardly a trace can be found. The deeper facets of the arts are missing in action. Think of the movies, for example. Although not all martial arts movies are quite as bad as I may have implied earlier, it is undeniable that the philosophy and the subtle beauty of the arts don't come across very well on the screen.

Clearly, part of the problem is to be found in the spectacular nature at the roots of the entertainment industry. Not only movies and video games creators, but also the news media know that in order to capture the public's short attention span, they better give them something loud, explosive and spectacular. Unfortunately, it just so happens that a wonderful philosophical approach to life is not very spectacular. Peace is not spectacular. And the reality of martial arts in the daily lives of thousands of practitioners doesn't seem very spectacular either. They may be deep, powerful and beautiful beyond words, but they don't translate well onto a screen. On the other hand, violence, action and furious fighting fit the bill perfectly. They are graphic, shocking and ideal to titillate the voyeuristic pleasures of a passive audience. They scream for the viewers' attention in a way that no philosophy will ever be able to do. Martial arts, therefore, work well on the screen only as long as they are willing to appear as a circus of screaming acrobats or as a bare-handed version of a Western movie.

The unfortunate aspect of martial arts' public image is that the media are the main source of information about martial arts for the vast majority of people. This is perhaps why some strange individuals sometimes come through the doors of martial arts schools. In their stereotypes-filled heads, they come having clear expectations of what martial arts are supposed to be like and seeking lessons hoping to emulate what they have seen on the screen.

Among those willing to sign up and put their money on the table are often two very different kinds of people. On one hand, there are the wannabe killing machines wishing to add martial skills to their already inflated egos. On the other, are those who have been seduced by one of the secondary themes in the martial arts movie genre that I have so far neglected to mention: the halo of spirituality surrounding Asian fighting arts. Mostly made of dialogues paraphrasing the messages of fortune cookies, this sub-genre captivates those individuals craving some kind of spiritual experience, no matter how shallow it may be. After watching David Carradine's *Kung Fu* TV series far too many times, the aspiring peaceful warriors approach martial arts schools hoping to learn from a wise Asian master how to develop mystical Chi powers while getting rid of giant bullies at the same time. Although the latter category of lunatic romantics is much more pleasant to deal with than the former, it is equally misguided and misinformed about the nature of martial arts.

In addition to being confused regarding the goals of martial arts practice, members of both categories are equally clueless regarding the physical techniques employed in martial arts. They have watched enough Hong Kong flicks that they believe they know what good fighting looks like. What unfortunately they forget is that the martial techniques shown at the theater often have little to do with real martial arts. In movies, the techniques are picked for their scenic effect, not for their effectiveness. Good luck to the guy who tries to survive a street fight thanks to flying kicks and acrobatic moves six feet up in the air. Used to the flashy techniques employed by movie-martial artists, they are puzzled when they walk into a school and what they see doesn't correspond to the moves pulled off by Keanu Reeves in *The Matrix*.

Enough with the complaints, Bolelli. Leave us alone and let us enjoy the show. Movies are movies. If you want realism, look at reality and save the price of the ticket.

Fair enough. I stand corrected and I'll quit whining about the stereotypical images of martial arts created by the media. After all, complaining and criticizing, however legitimate it may be, doesn't solve anything and gets boring very quickly. Although it is true that certain portraits of martial arts may create endless confusion, the problem exists only for those who expect to find realism in an entertainment product. This is not what movies are for. Movies, however, can move (please forgive the unintended pun) and inspire. Movies serve a powerful function by capturing the audience, stimulating their hearts, and planting seeds of desire in their minds.

Let's look again at the example of martial arts movies. If they are made of such useless, unrealistic junk, why do they fascinate so many people? Is it because they are action-packed and spectacular? Of course that's part of the reason, but is that all? Although I don't believe that popularity is a great indicator of depth, I suspect that even in the case of the lowest, most squalid B-movies, something deeper is at play. Ice-skating and platform diving are spectacular, action-packed events, but they are not exactly very popular, and no one would dream of making a movie genre of them.

Martial arts movies speak a language that is not simply spectacular, but powerful. The archetypal hero of martial arts movies is a warrior whose mastery of physical conflict allows him to escape from the lower levels of the food chain. Fighting is his art form. This is not a minor detail. As any successful producer, director and writer knows (including people like Shakespeare and the authors of the Old Testament), violence—along with sex—is the most international and oldest language there is. It is common to all societies. It is attached to the very fabric of life. Depending on their fighting ability (and on their culinary preferences), every animal on earth ends up taking on the role of predator or prey. Not only nearly all animals fight, but even the cells inside our bodies fight against germs and bacteria. No one who lives in a physical body can completely ignore the language of violence. Whether by choice or not, anyone may have to deal with it.

In addition to physical confrontations, symbolic forms of fighting between reality and individual desires are the daily bread of anyone who is alive. The physical violence that the hero of martial arts movies has to deal with is the most dramatic example of something that everyone experiences in daily life: conflict. Conflict with friends, lovers, people who cut you off in traffic. Internal conflict with one's laziness, weakness and lack of discipline. Conflict between desires and possibilities. Conflict between dreams and closed doors.

Conflict between one's ideals and one's behavior. Heraclitus was right when he said that conflict is at the root of all things.

Besides providing cheap entertainment, the hero fighting in martial arts movies is attractive because it reminds us of our own fights and provides precious inspiration. The game usually begins with evil ruling and no hope in sight. Just when everything seems lost, the hero's strong moral principles, coupled with bravery and willingness to act, force him to stand up for those who can't stand up for themselves. The same qualities without which the hero can't succeed on the screen—the same virtues of extreme willpower, tenacity, and refusal to give in to defeat under any circumstance— are the ones we need in our own personal struggles. Martial heroes in movies are strong, confident when all around them are scared, able to stay hopeful in the midst of desperation, daring in the face of overwhelming odds. Whereas weaker men would be crushed by the initial lack of success that nearly always awaits martial heroes on the screen, they remain focused and push themselves harder. No matter what setbacks they run into, they never die. They can be knocked-down—and they often are—but they are never knocked-out. Each time they hit the ground apparently defeated and bloodied, they find the power to get back up. Without these qualities, the hero would meet a premature end and happiness would be impossible to reach.

This is perhaps the reason why martial heroes appeal to so many people. The glamorous settings, the unrealistic stories, and the fast-paced action provide the colorful elements that are necessary to keep the viewers awake. But at the core of a martial arts movie— no matter how poorly done it may be—is the quest for power, the hero's journey to develop the qualities that can remove all the obstacles on the way to happiness. This is why if the movie is even remotely decent we can still benefit from watching it since it reminds us of the qualities we want to embody. In this sense, the martial hero stands as a model and an inspiration for daily life.

Whether they are conscious of it or not, this is one of the forces pulling viewers in front of the screen. Sadly, many people are thrilled as long as the film is rolling, but as soon as the two hours of entertainment are over they forget all about heroic virtues and go back to being their pathetic selves. Which leaves me wondering: what's the point of being inspired by something if you don't do anything with it? The separation between passive entertainment and real life is as sharp as it could be. However, it doesn't have to be. Movies, like martial arts practice itself, could be approached as rituals to get in touch with the heroic qualities we cherish, and help us remember the sacred fire laying dormant within.

Of course, being able to view martial arts movies as sacred rituals is much easier said than done. The quality level of many of them is so low that it is hard to watch them with a straight face. This is not to say that all of them are equally bad. Contrary to what I may have suggested at the beginning of this chapter, some are actually pretty good movies. *Fist of Legend,* for example, starring Chinese Wushu champion turned actor Jet Li, is a beautiful remake of one of the movies that did most to popularize the martial arts movie genre: Bruce Lee's *Chinese Connection.* Loosely based on historical events, *Fist of Legend* is set during the Japanese occupation of China in the first part of the twentieth century, and follows the story of a famous kung fu school targeted by the Japanese invaders. In addition to the fact that it is splendidly shot and that it adds spice to the original plot in a variety of ways, the appeal of *Fist of Legend* rests with Jet Li's excellent performance as a quiet but tremendously confident hero. Some scenes, in particular, stand out as examples of martial poetry. At one point of the movie, the plot slows down long enough to give space to a wonderful scene of martial brotherhood, as Jet Li and his favorite training partner, after they had a bloody falling out, reunite to chat in front of a fire at night. Their minds heavy with the choices they'll soon have to face, the two begin showing each other the techniques they have been working on and soon forget about everything else, consumed by the sheer joy of training. Despite its brevity, the scene is a beautiful window which tells more about the spirit of martial arts than any spectacular fighting scene.

Although Bruce Lee's own movies are now quite dated, are responsible for many of the stereotypes later exploited by the martial arts movie genre, and don't render full justice to the philosophical depth that Lee was capable of, they nonetheless offer some powerful moments. Lee's intensity coupled with the occasional blessing from the goddess of philosophy have managed to keep me going back to them time after time.

In recent times, regardless of what one may think of the Chinese passion for flying characters with a bad relationship with the laws of physics, *Crouching Tiger-Hidden Dragon* has been a film of tremendous importance. It courageously took martial arts away from the niche of B-movies and presented them in an unusual artistic cloak. Controversial and out of the ordinary, *Crouching Tiger-Hidden Dragon* shows a very different side to the traditional character of martial heroes. Female fighters in love with sensitive Mongolian outlaws, flying fights over bamboo trees, waterfalls and lakes, tough martial artists struggling over the waste caused by too many rules and unexpressed love. Like the movie or hate it, director Ang Lee's amazing sensitivity for evocative, poetic images has brought the quality of martial arts movies up by several notches.

Speaking of cinematographic genius, only by going back in time it is possible to find another rare example of a martial arts script in the hands of director who was kissed by the Muse. In 1942, shortly after Bruce Lee had cartwheeled out of his mother's womb, long before the martial arts movie genre ever became a genre, the man who would become the god of Japanese cinema made his debut with a film about the fighting career of one of Kodokan Judo's early legends. *Sanshiro Sugata* by Akira Kurosawa, based on the life-story of the formidable judoka Shiro Saigo, is one of those rare pearls combining a glorious use of the camera with a martial arts subject. For those brave movie-watching mavericks who are not scared off by the presence of subtitles and black-and-white, *The Seven Samurai* is one of Kurosawa's other masterpieces dedicated to martial arts lore.

Isolated and far-between, these examples shine because of their uniqueness. They are happy oases in the middle of the artistic waste-land that gives birth to most martial arts movies. This, however, doesn't deter me from digging in the trash to find a few good mar-tial scenes. Rather, I happily choose to dive into the bizarre world of B-movies where martial arts have built their cinematographic home. What I want, in fact, is to be moved and inspired. If I can silence my critical voice long enough to get there by watching the worst, trashy movie on the planet, so be it. I have no complaints. Being too smart in this case is not wise. The movie, after all, is just a mean to an end. I would rather get passionate and motivated because of a stupid movie than not get passionate at all. Whatever works is fine for me. So long as I can avoid falling prey to cynicism, maybe I can still get the result I am looking for. Sometimes, of course, that's just not possible. Many martial arts movies are sim-ply too bad for me to endure. But if I can help it, I try to leave my intellectual palate at home and have no qualms about being inspired by the trash. However well hidden and disguised, the myth lives even in the worst Van Damme movie. This is why my myth-craving stomach feasts on appetizers of Mark Dacascos, salads of Chuck Norris, and main courses of Steven Seagal.

The warrior myth that is at the roots of martial arts, however, is not found only in what corresponds to a narrow definition of a martial arts movie. *The Star Wars* original trilogy serves as a good example. *Star Wars, The Empire Strikes Back,* and *The Return of the Jedi* are three sci-fi films, full of special effects, good and evil robots, aliens of all shapes and forms, and imperial spaceships fighting rebel spaceships. But this is not all. They also are three martial arts movies that focus on the warrior myth much more than many orthodox martial arts flicks. The characters of Yoda and Obi Wan Kenobi are molded on the archetype of the Taoist fighting mas-ters. The "Force," the invisible energy that gives life to all things and that can be tapped into as a source of incredible powers, is taken directly from the concept of Chi existing in the lore of Asian martial arts. The martial and philosophical training of the Jedi Knights has some parallels in those schools of martial arts where the formation of a complete individual goes hand in hand with the development of fighting skills.

Girlfight is a recent independent film by writer/director Karyn Kusama centered on the character of Diana Guzman, splendidly interpreted by Michelle Rodriguez. If faithfully following the Judeo-Christian tradition you believe that women came into being because our good God wanted to entertain Adam, don't go tell Diana Guzman. The protection of only one God would not be enough to keep your bones in one piece. Diana Guzman is not the kind of girl who buys so-called women's magazines teaching her how to use make-up, when to diet, and where to buy fashionable clothes. She is not a Marilyn Monroe whose world turns around the conquest of a man. She is not a damsel in distress needing to be saved by the hero of the story. She is not a cheerleader waiting on the sideline to boost the hero's ego. She is a Latina teenager with fire in her eyes, annoyed by the squalor of high-school life and pissed-off with the world, who challenges everything and everybody in order to learn how to box. Her story is pure muscular epic. Watching her sweat and fight one training session after another is to bear witness to the determination and steel discipline required of a martial artist. Throughout the movie, Guzman pushes herself, unwilling to make up alibis for her failings or take no for an answer. Although the art of choice here is boxing, the movie speaks a language that should be very familiar to any martial artist and to anyone with the courage to mould their own character and carve their own destiny.

If the parallels between the martial arts and movies like the *Star Wars* trilogy and *Girlfight* are not so hard to find, we have to stretch the flexibility of our definitions a little further to see how *Conan the Barbarian* (possibly the most individualistic movie in history, and certainly the only one combining quotations from Nietzsche, Genghis Khan and anonymous Apache warriors) or Disney's *Mulan* can be considered martial arts movies. But if we stop looking at the letter of martial arts and focus on the spirit of what martial arts really are, that shouldn't be so hard to do. The warrior myth eats and breathes around the campfires of martial artists, but is not caged there. The warrior myth is more about the burning of a sacred fire under one's skin than it is about the performance of exotic-looking fighting techniques. Whoever can put on the screen that type of spirit is making a movie about the essence of martial arts, whether it shows any martial arts or not. In my book, good martial arts movies are not always about martial arts.

Unfortunately, the warrior myth does not enjoy much credit among the more sensitive fringes of moviegoers. Viewed as a macho fantasy and fit only for Neanderthal-like people with more muscles than brain, the warrior myth is seen by some (in particular by women) as an unimaginative cheap thrill for equally cheap people. This—I believe—is a costly mistake. From the *Lord of the Rings* to Bruce Lee, from *the Big Wednesday* to Kurosawa, from *Star Wars* to the cave paintings of Paleolithic hunters, the warrior myth has been an integral part of human nature. The details of the story and the quality of the representation may vary, but the heart is always the same. The near-sightedness of much of European cultural and political thought has labeled the figure of the strong individual as a right-winged phenomenon. Although American culture is not as polarized by the division between right-winged and left-winged as European culture is (perhaps because so many Americans don't know the first thing about politics,) this way of thinking has to a certain degree permeated some parts of American thought as well. Animated by the best intentions, many yoga-practicing, organic tofu-eating, politically very correct pacifists throughout the world have followed suit and have similarly cast a critical eye on the warrior myth and regarded it as a right-winged fantasy. Stories centered on a powerful hero—they say—are right-winged. Magical cultures and knights-tales are right-winged. Right-winged are Nietzsche and Tolkien. Right-winged is the act of daring and being brave. Right-winged is any form of individualism. Right-winged is the cult of strength and willpower. Right-winged are those who chase utopias and dare to escape their dull, social obligations. Right-winged is any fantasy challenging the limitations of the surrounding reality. Labeling all these things as right-winged, however, is the silly superstition of a mediocre and rigidly rational ideology that mistakenly attributes to right-winged thought a beauty that has nothing to do with political doctrines.

The warrior myth doesn't belong to any political ideology. It is for all human beings. The warrior myth has been imprinted in our DNA thousands of years ago, long before the categories of left-wing and right-wing were ever invented. Myths are nothing but faces of human experience. If the figure of the fighting hero has been so deeply entrenched in the imagination of our ancestors and has not stopped fascinating us even today is because it talks in a language that our souls understand well. The Myth talks about our life. It is something that we need as much as oxygen and water because air and food feed the body but the myth keeps character alive.

Too often we treat movies, music and books as forms of entertainment designed to lend a little bit of color to our daily lives, a pastime in which our only role is that of spectators. We are intrigued for a few hours and that's the end of it. But the myth doesn't want to be passively received, and it certainly doesn't want to be studied or analyzed. It wants to be lived out. The technical details of a book, a piece of music, or a film, are not all that important. What matters is if the book, the song or the movie can inspire us to follow our highest hopes and remind us of what Nietzsche called "the hero hidden in your soul." This is the function of myth. It reminds us of our dreams. It reminds us of the individual we wish to be so that we don't end up opening our eyes one morning, in the year 2037, only to find out that too many years of our life have gone by, and we haven't lived, we haven't given birth to our visions and have never had experiences deserving to be written with gold clouds in the sky.

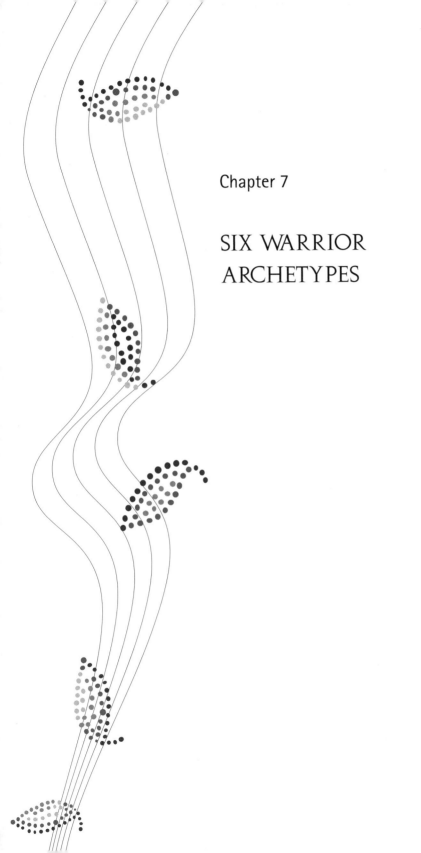

Chapter 7

SIX WARRIOR
ARCHETYPES

Six faces of the warrior myth. Individuals who lived where history turns into epic poetry. Gone beyond the boundaries of time that can be measured by watches, hourglasses, and calendars. Six costumes in the fighting gods' wardrobe. There are still places where you can hear the wind telling about their feats. On the hills around a river called Little Bighorn, the drums of thousands of Cheyenne and Lakota hunters never stopped playing. The eyes of warriors who turned to dust hundreds of years ago still shine in the fog of the Iga mountains. Centuries-old tracks mark the floor of a Buddhist temple in the Henan Province. There is magic in the air. A magic that whispers in your ears and gets under your muscles. The magic of lands which have not forgotten what they witnessed. But the spirits of those who fought for their visions don't dwell only in those places. A spark of them is in the heart of every human being who knows what it means to live as a warrior. The six fighters coming to visit us today are inspirational figures: mythological images to meditate upon. I can see them as the Major Arcana in the tarot deck of martial arts. Six archetypal energies. Six ways to face conflict. If we are ready to accept them, each one of them will bring us two gifts, offering us the sources of their power and also warning us about their own weaknesses. For those who know how to see beyond the pages of the history books, here are six masters of the way of the warrior.

THE SAMURAI

There are things for which it is worth losing everything: things that are worth more than fame, more than power, more than any kind of wealth; things that separate normal human beings from those individuals whose will cannot be broken by external events. Two swords and a set of armor don't make a samurai. Not even great martial skill and membership in a renowned family of warriors are enough. It is not a question of technique or heritage. A samurai is one who forges his spirit according to the ways of Bushido.

No word is strong enough to define what Bushido means to a

samurai. In comparison, the promises of eternal love between two lovers and the devotion of a priest for his God are but small things. Love can end and a dying faith can be traded in for a new one. Bushido is a different story. Bushido is the soul of the samurai, the vibrant heart that instills power into his every action. The Japanese samurai of the past lived their existence following a chivalrous code of behavior which didn't leave any room for compromise. No "buts," no "ifs." Bushido has no patience for exceptions. The samurai were taught since they were very young never to play with their principles. One mistake, just one moment of weakness when their honor may be slightly compromised, and *harakiri* knocks at the door. Twelve inches of steel to be stuck in one's abdomen in an act of ritual suicide can be a very convincing argument. It is therefore natural that people whose way of saying "Sorry, I made a mistake" was harakiri, would take their ideals very seriously.

Contrary to what certain stereotypes say, the samurai is not masochist nor is he suicidal. Like any other human being the samurai loves life, but the difference is that to him a life without honor is not worth living. Everyday life offers us many chances to run across people who spend their existences hiding, looking for justifications. People without the courage to risk an inch of security to follow their visions. People without pride or character. Around one who is ready to follow one's visions at any price, instead, it is possible to sense a dignity beyond words. In the eyes of a samurai one can see a kind of sincerity that is unknown to those who live chasing alibis: the sincerity of one who can't lie to himself by making up excuses. Pretending from himself a perfection that goes beyond human limits and putting all of his energies into every action are his way of living. A will charged at an extremely high voltage and an implacable determination never abandon him, because every matter is a matter of life or death. One mistake is one too many.

A samurai doesn't forget. He doesn't ask for anybody's help, but is ready to tame storms for those who give him their trust. The person who holds out a hand to help him, gains an ally willing to die to return the favor. Betraying one who has given him their heart is not an option for a samurai. Even the power of laws and written contracts fade in comparison with his word, because laws can be bent with shrewdness and contracts can be broken, but his word is more sacred than life itself. The samurai is much more than a formidable warrior. He is the embodiment of a depth of feelings transcending Japanese history and culture. He is a symbol of the integrity, the power and the beauty that are accessible to any human being who has the courage to be faithful to oneself.

But like all medicines, even the Bushido can turn into poison if taken in massive dosage. Historically, the majority of samurai were far from being noble, romantic figures. For great numbers of samurai, the total determination to follow one's code of honor turned into obsessive fanaticism. The armor got the upper hand over the man: no smiles, no sense of humor. So busy chasing perfection as to forget to breathe. Relax, man, lighten up. There is no need to be rigid in order to conserve our honor. Animated by such strong passion as to be ready to die for our ideals, but without enough passion to be truly alive.

When a samurai loses balance, strength turns into stiffness and the bushido turns into a prison. Honor ceases to be the quality of an extraordinary individual and is transformed into a fascist perversion. Even the faithfulness to those who trust in him becomes a justification for being a killer at the service of warlords and of an oppressive social order. A dogmatic soldier without feelings. It is the takeover of rules enslaving the man who created them and pushing him to become the servant of a death machine with no room for human qualities. It is not easy to keep such a delicate balance between on one side, a sublime spiritual stature, and on the other, the loss of one's humanity. Ueshiba wrote a beautiful thing to remind the samurai of the original sense of Bushido: "The true meaning of the term samurai is one who serves and adheres to the power of love."

THE NINJA

Three hundred and sixty degrees away from the samurai lives the ninja. Both his powers and his weaknesses are opposite to those of the samurai. The ninja is the outlaw, the anarchist, the iconoclast. The philosophical conflict between ninja and samurai is a universal theme, in feudal Japan just as among Homeric heroes. Aiax is a samurai. Ulysses is a ninja. Aiax, an unshakable mountain, full of pride and of his boundless strength, ready to fight face to face against an entire army. Ulysses, a shadow warrior, strikes when the night is dark and disappears before sunrise. He doesn't need to fight where the battle is fiercest to demonstrate his courage. Silent and unseen, he achieves what ten thousand warriors charging straightforward cannot accomplish.

The ninja doesn't acknowledge any authority to laws alien to his heart. "I didn't create them—he declares—I don't subscribe to them. So I don't have to live by them." The samurai looks at the ninja with contempt, considering him nothing more than a nocturnal predator without honor or morals. But the samurai is wrong. It isn't that the ninja has no morals. Simply, he is not bound by rules written in stone. His morals have their sources in the paradoxical waters of Taoism. He doesn't dogmatically apply a series of preset rules and, like Tom Robbins' outlaws, doesn't need to consult a manual of good behavior to decide what to do.

The ninja chooses to choose. Always. Every situation is unique and should be faced as such. Neither human nor divine laws can choose for him. Faced with the events of life, he stays open, flexible. The legend tells that the ninjas were born from family clans that lived in the mountains far away from the headquarters of the central government, in small communities that had abandoned the social order in order to dedicate themselves to the creation of an autonomous culture. Ninja philosophy—myths say—had its origin in the meeting of some exiled Chinese warrior-shamans and groups of Japanese families who had no intention to remain within the dominant feudal society. From the syncretism of certain aspects of Tibetan Tantrism, Taoist texts on the art of war, and some yogic techniques belonging to secret sects of Buddhism, they created a vision of life radically different from the ideals of medieval Japan. When society decided to crack down on the lifestyles of these mystics of the mountains, the ninjas used their skills to defend themselves and turned into indomitable warriors.

Ninjas didn't fight for glory and didn't have a reputation to defend, so they also didn't have any scruples about using every possible mean to protect their families and their lifestyles. If the ninjas had fought in the open against an enemy who enjoyed a vast numerical superiority, they would have been blown away. So, in order to come out on top, the ninjas had no qualms about rewriting the rules of the game. No unnecessary risks. No foolish bravado. Accomplish what you need to accomplish and disappear before being discovered. Physical and psychological guerrilla warfare was the ninja way to give battle.

The myth speaks of the ninjas as cultural heroes, mystic outlaws, tribal Robin Hoods. But there is also a second historical reality to the ninjas. Because of the great effectiveness of the ninjas, the warlords hired anyone whose moral reservations were weaker than their loyalty as mercenaries, special agents to be used for those tasks going beyond the ethical limits of the samurai. However, the line between outlaw and criminal shouldn't be crossed lightly. One breaks society's laws but is faithful to his own code of honor. The other has little honor to speak of and is willing to do anything for material advantages. The ninjas of the myth—freedom-fighting outlaws animated by a deep philosophical vision of the universe—didn't always find embodiment in the actual historical ninjas, who were often little other than killers without principles for whom success justified any means. The delicate Taoist relativism of the former was absolute relativism for the latter. The border between the flexibility of a mystic and the cynicism of a criminal is what stands between the dark and the light side of the ninja.

The ninja and the samurai are the opposite poles of a perfect antithesis, but they both draw water from deep sources of power and they both can turn into horrible mutations with no resemblance to their potential splendor. Hidden in a philosophical forest, somewhere halfway between the ideal of the samurai and that of the ninja is a warrior who knows how to escape the slavery of moral imperatives without turning into a mercenary without any dignity.

THE SEARCHERS

As King Arthur would say, "Now once more I must ride with my knights to defend what was and the dream of what could be." The romanticism surrounding the myth of the band of mystic heroes fighting to right all wrongs has always created legendary figures. They are the Shaolin fighting monks, the Knights of the Round Table, the Jedi masters, or the members of the Fellowship of the Ring. They heard the Call and followed it until they met each other. The search united them in a pact of spiritual brotherhood between seekers of intensity.

Belonging to a tribe of searchers is always the result of a choice. Nobody is born a Shaolin monk or a Knight of the Round Table. Listening to the Call is the way to become one of them. It is one of the most classical warrior myths to ever touch the heart of our collective imagination: the elite group of heroes bound together by a common mission.

Like true warrior-gentlemen, the group of seekers is busy on two fronts. On one side there is the inner search whose goal is the Grail of personal enlightenment; a constant quest for self-perfection pushing them not to settle for the goals ordinary men dream of. On the other side there is the path of the fighting bodhisatva. In the Mahaparinivvana-sutra is written: "If enlightening beings practice mundane tolerance and thus do not stop evil people, allowing them to increase in evil ..., then these enlightening beings are actually devils, not enlightening beings." Among monks as well as knights, this feeling finds wide support. In many parts of the world neither saw any contradiction between dedicating oneself to spirituality with body and soul, and fighting against all forms of evil. Actually, for them fighting against anything upsetting the natural harmony of life was the direct consequence of a spiritual vision of the world. Martial arts were nothing but an extension of spirituality. Religion, philosophy, healing techniques and martial arts were all branches of the same tree designed to improve the overall quality of life.

But the ghost of self-righteous fanaticism knocks on the door. The combination of a sense of religious duty and fighting instincts can pave the way for some very unhealthy tendencies. The picture of the missionary with Bible in one hand and rifle in the other is one of the fundamentalist perversions born from a bad mix of spirituality and warrior philosophy. There is nothing worse than those who are willing to chop heads off because they feel like they are on a mission from God. Feeling that their way is the Only True Way and that anyone not following it is an agent of evil forces, the religious warriors often don't have many reservations about slaughtering those who choose different values. The Shaolin monks' Buddhist wisdom and the poetic complicity of the narrators of King Arthur's saga prevented them from falling prey to any fundamentalist frenzy. But the Christian crusaders, the Islamic suicide-bombers and Reverend Jones' disciples remind us of what happens when the searchers get lost.

THE HERMIT

Only a few lines for the hermit, because he doesn't like the company of too many words. If there were a church of the martial arts, the hermits would be its saints. Very little is known about them. Mystery surrounds them. But at the genesis of many martial arts, there is the figure of the hermit. He arrives at dawn before a martial art has any history. His story is murky, like the appearance of a ghost who passes on the treasures of his knowledge before disappearing again in the fog. History begins only after a travelling warrior stumbles upon one of these mystics of the forest, shares for several years the hermit's solitude by becoming his disciple, and then comes back in the world to teach what he has learned.

In the Chinese martial tradition, the hermit is often a lonely Taoist who lives on the mountains in the company of the animals and the natural elements. Nature teaches him the ways of enlightenment and immortality. Observing wild animals dueling, he learns fighting techniques unknown to human beings. Worldly affairs have no importance for him because he stepped away from history in order to dance with eternity. He lives in a parallel world that doesn't follow the same laws of human society. He doesn't belong anymore to what is commonly identified as humanity.

This is his gift as well as his danger. A shamanic story tells that it is very easy for apprentices who learn to travel from a human body into a deer's body to be unable to come back to the human level. Often, the lack of experience makes them forget to buy the return ticket. Shamans say that in the consciousness of a deer there is no desire to enter into a human body, so some badly prepared apprentices remain stuck forever. Ascending so high as to forget the earth is the danger of the hermit who loses his balance. Too much power can blind. Rather than learning how to move between two worlds, he takes a one-way trip for a nirvana which has no place for the soft embrace of a wonderful woman, or for a Pearl Jam concert.

THE RONIN

The dictionary tells us that the ronin is a samurai who doesn't serve any master. But as an archetype, the ronin is the symbol of something much broader: something that is not limited to Japanese history and traditions. It is a universal image. Every epoch and every culture has seen the spirit of the ronin being born under different shapes. The mountain man who ventures alone to live as a hunter before the lands of North America became states. The knight whose sword doesn't obey the orders of a king, but only those of his heart. The freelance gunfighter that nobody can trust but that everyone wants on their side. Even the hackers, the computer-cowboys who roam around the prairies of cyberspace. Rimbaud is a ronin and so is Fitzcarraldo. A nomadic warrior who doesn't stop in any place long enough to grow roots. He offers his services to the highest bidder before disappearing again following a different trail. He is an anarchist adventurer in the best case, and a mercenary in the worse.

Nietzsche writes, "One must still have chaos in oneself to be able to give birth to a dancing star." Unnecessary words for the ronin, since chaos is his natural lifestyle. He is not the kind of man who can live by the routine of a regular job and who goes on holiday with the family for the weekend. One can't expect him to be on time with mortgage payments on the home. Maybe it is more precise to say that he doesn't even know what a home is. In his DNA are the genes of the genius as well as those of the beast. The chaos of his spirit is the sun illuminating his life as well as the curse that can ruin him.

At any moment, you could find him dead in an alley after a squalid brawl between drunken smugglers, but just as likely you could find him at the head of an empire. Chance plays dice with his destiny. One minute it looks like there is nothing despicable enough that he wouldn't do for the right price. The next moment he is ready to give up an economic fortune going beyond anyone's wildest dreams in the name of some dangerous, idealistic enterprise. It is impossible to predict what his next move will be. The only certain thing is that one never gets bored staying around him.

The ronin is the meteor of the warrior tradition. He doesn't have history or parents, and was never schooled by anyone. Saying that he is independent is a mild euphemism. He created himself: a mushroom spore fallen on earth from outer space. He lives in the world, in the midst of action, but he is more lonesome than the loneliest hermit on the mountains. His heart doesn't belong to anybody and he is far too weird for anyone to follow him. No rational being would follow him to dance on a rope stretched above the precipice. But he doesn't stop to reflect, doesn't ponder and makes no plans. Without thoughts or fear, the ronin dances just a step away from the abyss.

THE TRIBAL WARRIOR

June 25, 1876, state of Montana. Thousands of Cheyenne and Lakota warriors have gone to face the column of soldiers who wanted to attack them. They crushed them and took away from them any enthusiasm for battle. While on the hills the Indians chase the last soldiers trying to run away, another threat steps onto the scene. A second group of almost 300 soldiers has arrived in the valley from the opposite side and is getting ready to attack the women, the elders and the children left alone in the completely defenseless camp. Almost completely defenseless. Four Cheyenne warriors who didn't take part in the first fight are still in camp. A few seconds are enough to understand that the thousands of warriors on the hills will not arrive in time to defend the camp before the soldiers attack. The four Cheyenne take a look at the camp that in just a few minutes may turn into a slaughterhouse, look each other in the eyes, and without any hesitation pick up their weapons, jump on their horses and charge against General Custer's two hundred sixty-three cavalry men. Their uninterrupted fire slows down the advance of the soldiers, buying time for the other warriors to come down from the hills at full gallop and swallow Custer in a single mouthful.

It is not easy to be a tribal warrior. There is little to gain for one's actions: not much power and not much wealth; no personal profit justifying the risks a warrior must face. If there is no material incentive, what then pushes a person to silence the voice of their own survival instinct? What pushes four men to charge into battle against two hundred sixty-three? The answer can be found in one of the Sun Dance songs which are still sung to this day when, during the summer's most important ritual of the North American Plains tribes, the men have their chests pierced and dance for four days without food or water.

Oyate yanipikta cha
   (So that) The people will live
Leca mu welo.
   That is why I do this.

The power of the warrior in tribal societies comes from his people. The warrior is the shield protecting the whole tribe. He hunts for those who don't have any food. He defends those who are too weak to defend themselves. No one, not even the bravest warrior is without fear. But there are things that are much more important than fear and death. There is the tribe. When a warrior remembers his people, fear loses its grip on him. It is said that Crazy Horse, one of the most famous Lakota tribal heroes, several times spurred his horse toward dozens of enemies in order to save a wounded friend. These things are hard to understand for people who dedicate more time to earning money than to cultivating friendships; people who are part of a society that has forgotten that human nature is tribal.

The irrational fascination that many non-Indian peoples feel for American Indians goes—at least sometimes—beyond the folklore of eagle feathers, war-paint and exotic names. It is the longing for a more human lifestyle, not ruled by the rhythm of production. No clock telling us when to eat, when to sleep, or when it is time to have fun. No rush hour on the way to an office. The office is the woods and prairies, those places now flocked by thousands of tourists paying top money for the privilege to spend a weekend there.

And then there is the tribal structure. Beyond what we know as friendship. Individuals who have known you since birth, individuals ready to die for you, ready to give you anything they have if you are ever in need. As long as one eats, everyone eats. Give and receive, give and receive. For the majority of human history, all peoples throughout the world lived in tribes. The loneliness, the alienation, the desire for a community plaguing millions of people today are the direct result of having lost the key to tribal living.

Anyone having a living heart knows that inside our chests beat the echo of a tribal nostalgia.

But even the tribal warrior—just as tribal societies in general—has a dark side. The danger of the tribe is the closing of one's options, the isolation from the rest of the world, the creation of an "Us vs. Them" mentality based on which group one is born into. The warrior can be so caught up with what is happening in his tribe as not to be able to see beyond the borders of his own camp. Anyone who is not part of the tribe is seen as a potential enemy. If you are not with us, you are against us. Moreover, the tribe itself can be a stifling force which enforces consensus by looking suspiciously on the flow of new ideas and by castigating those who dare to think along different lines. The greatest challenge for the tribal warrior is to learn the secrets of a consciousness that is tribal and cosmic at the same time.

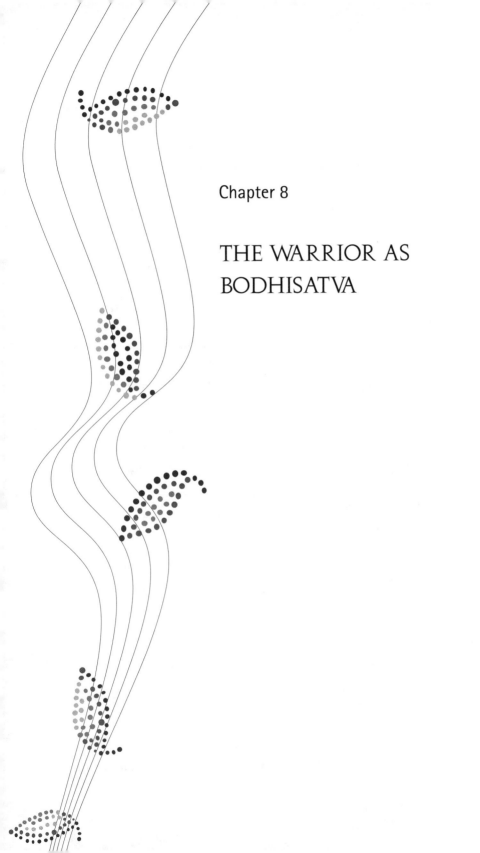

Chapter 8

THE WARRIOR AS BODHISATVA

No matter how much pleasure I derive from martial arts training, nagging questions periodically resurface. Why do we fight? What do we seek in the martial arts? What are we training for? Which primordial call pushes our bodies and minds to undergo hundreds of hours of practice? Yes, martial arts training can be incredibly fun and enjoyable. But are a little fun and enjoyment all that we are really looking for? In the vast majority of cases, I'm afraid they are. For many people, the goal is learning how to fight in order to defeat their fears and gain some measure of self-confidence. Some are simply bored out of their minds and want a hobby to distract them from the monotony of their lives. Sculpting their bodies into temples dedicated to health and strength is the aim of those hooked on fitness and physical wellbeing. Others are enraptured by aesthetic beauty and wish to create poetry through the movements of their bodies. For others still, martial arts are an inner path of self-discovery aimed at learning how to live calmly, in peace, beyond conflict.

I hope I don't come across as arrogant, but I believe that even the best of these goals are little more than side benefits. Although they stand as the ultimate aims of training for ninety-nine percent of martial artists, I can't help seeing them only as the tools needed before the real game can begin. Clearly, all these choices are legitimate and essential. Molding our characters in order to become more gracious people in everyday life is already more than most people dream of doing. I would have never written the preceding chapters if I didn't have great respect for the people who approach martial arts with these intentions. But my feeling is that something much bigger is at stake. Idealism? Perhaps. But why should we settle for limited goals when so much more is within reach?

Once we have given shape to a body which moves with grace and power wherever it is—once we are at peace with ourselves, our minds are clear and we feel rivers of internal strength and love for life flowing in our veins—why should we choose to return to our nine to five world and channel all this energy into aseptic, lifeless environments hundreds of miles away from our inner beauty?

Do the treasures we have found along the way serve only to make us more efficient on the job and our existence just a little more bearable? The inner strength, willpower and confidence that martial arts can bring would be better used for something much more radical than just providing a little help in our daily lives. I am aware of taking a step in a direction that not many martial artists are ready to follow. But my vision tells me that if the way of the warrior doesn't give birth to a spiritual revolution shaking the very roots of our way of facing life, we might as well flush it.

I love martial arts. I love their power. I love their beauty. I love hearing the sound made by the heart of a warrior ... boom ... boom ... moved not by inertia, but by passion. Every beat echoes the magic of being alive. I love the romanticism of warrior legends. I love the way in which the warrior challenges his own limits. I love the way he smiles when faced by what normal people call impossible. The courage of the warrior has nothing to do with displays of machismo or with the rhetoric of football coaches. It is the courage to take destiny in the palm of our hands and become the leader of our own lives, and this is what I love most of all.

The way of the warrior is not a hobby nor is it a collection of fighting techniques and physical exercises. It is a way to wake up, to walk, to drink, to think, to act. One who remembers to be a warrior only within the confines of a martial arts school is not a warrior at all. The sword master Seizan wrote, "The dojo is the background and everyday life comes first. Therefore, it is silly to think that it is sufficient to carry oneself well only in the dojo." If our way of being warriors is limited to the practice of martial arts, we haven't learned much. Cultivating warrior virtues is not a part-time job: heroes for two hours within a dojo, before going back to a life without magic. Everyday life is the real battlefield.

Martial arts are not important. What is important is who we are and what we want to become. Important are our dreams, our ideals, our lives, the kind of persons we would like to be. To be truly walking on the warrior's path, we have to bring our minds back to the time when we were not ashamed of our dreams; when reality had not yet frustrated our ambitions; when our desire was still too strong to be repressed, and our spirit refused to surrender in resignation; when we were not yet doctors, businessmen, or lawyers, but still wanted to be heroes, leaders, bodhisatvas. The first step on the way to being warriors is to get back in touch with our dreams.

A few years ago, I was talking with a journalist about a book I had co-authored in Italy *(Mitologie Felici.)* During the interview, I was asked if the figure of the hero still had some meaning in today's world, if contemporary culture still had room for the existence of people like Buddha, Crazy Horse, or the Knights of The Round Table. At that moment, the question didn't strike me as particularly meaningful, and I let it go without responding adequately. Only now, several years later, have I realized the importance of the question and have found the answer that I wish I had given. Thinking that the figure of the hero belongs to the past or to the kingdom of romantic fairytales is the biggest mistake we could make.

Open your eyes and look in any direction. The signs are everywhere. It is enough to take a deep breath to smell desperation. Every day, another piece of the planet we inhabit is destroyed. The voice of the Earth tells of forests being clear-cut, of the extinction of hundreds of species, of overpopulation, of the disappearance of natural resources, of poisons contaminating the air we breathe and the water we drink. The ecological condition of the Earth seems to have escaped from the apocalyptic nightmares of a biblical prophet who woke up in a particularly bad mood.

But this is only the reflection of our inner crisis. No ecosystem is as badly damaged as the hearts and the souls of human beings. The destruction is the product of a lost, wounded spirit that has forgotten how to live. We destroy anything crossing our path because we don't remember how to create. We have become hostages in the hands of the very system we have built. We devote most of our lives to jobs that don't make us dream or rejoice. We die a little everyday, accepting to sacrifice our desires in exchange for empty comforts and economic security. Occupying our time and filling our inner emptiness, materialism acts as an anesthetic. But from the poorest to the richest among us, anyone who works for something less than being caressed every day by the ecstasy of life, is nothing but a slave. There are billionaire slaves, slaves who control the political destiny of entire nations, and slaves who are famous and admired by other slaves.

Although maybe pleasant, ultimately wealth, fame, and power don't matter much. If our daily experience is not a source of happiness, we are still prisoners of our own existence. We have been raised in a society of unhappy people who have forgotten the beauty of being alive; thus, we deliver ourselves to the logic of profit and gain hoping that money can buy us our dreams. Schools and universities feed us to the mouth of the monster, boring us to death with studies devoid of life and warmth, inhibiting our natural creativity and preparing us to be swallowed up by the gloomy social structures. Often, our friendships, our relationships, our families, and even the houses in which we live and the food we eat are the reflections of the squalid life we find ourselves caged into. The nightmares of sleepy gods.

Confusion, insecurity, and self-destruction are the daily bread of millions of people. Every day seeds of unhappiness and sorrow are sown into the hearts of thousands of human beings. Every day, violence, alcohol, and drugs destroy as many people as do dullness, lack of creativity, boredom, and the shallowness of lives lived without flashes of intensity. Every day, mediocrity and resignation find their way into the spirits of human beings. They stifle us little by little, making us forget our true nature and turning us into the gears of an assembly-line producing sadness and destruction: shadows of our divine potential.

Anyone can see that we live in a sick society. But recognizing the disease is not enough. As Buddha says in the famous parable of the arrow, analyzing the disease is not nearly as important as finding a cure. Complaining about the state of things is a common sport. But who among us has the courage and the willpower to hold on to their dreams when everything around us tells us to give up? Who has the passion and the creative strength to reinvent our approach to life? We are surrounded by cynicism and abandonment. There are no Jedi masters guiding us along the way. Only a mass of faces on which are carved the wrinkles of defeat. We are left alone to confront reality, without anybody helping us to cultivate the warrior hidden in our souls.

The average level of self-confidence is so low that it should climb to the top of the Himalayas just to reach the navel of a gnome; but even if it weren't so, changing the destiny of the world would not be an easy task. Many people don't even attempt to take up the challenge, but prefer to surrender without fighting. The immensity of the task that lies ahead of us disheartens even the best of people. Faced with an undertaking of such gigantic proportions, we immediately become conscious of all the limitations of our individuality. The difficulties barring the way make us feel small and powerless. Kamikaze ants trying to stop a tank. Any effort seems to be in vain. But if we don't want to join the ranks of the living dead who simply endure life, it is better to stop complaining and expecting somebody else to find the solutions.

Today humankind has the potential to turn this planet into a paradise and live in beauty, just as it has the potential to destroy itself, the Earth and all living things. At stake in this game is our own individual existence, and the existence of humankind as a whole. What I have just described is not exactly a pretty picture, but my intention is not to depress, nor to advocate fatalism. Refusing to look at problems doesn't solve anything. It is healthy to stare the beast in the eyes. Pretending not to see it only because we are afraid of not being up to the challenge only acknowledges our defeat. Problems exist all around us. Big problems. Huge problems. Overwhelming problems. Terrifying problems. Problems with no apparent solution. The superficial creed of "everything is for the best" is a cope-out just as much as the pessimism of those who shrug their shoulders as they expose all the reasons why nothing can be done.

The fact that we are successfully flirting with self-destruction and that few people seem to care is not an encouraging sign. But let's not forget that nothing is predestined. The game is still very much alive. Right now is the time to lift our heads and show the power of our visions. As long as the spirit of a warrior lives in the heart of even just one of us, the dance is not over. Taking responsibility doesn't mean showing off our muscles or getting lost in visions of messianic omnipotence. Neither a teen-utopia nor the rhetoric of a Western movie, heroism is a matter of sensitivity. It is a yes to life. It means becoming a cultivator of happiness: doing the best to live in harmony and spread the contagion of harmony to those around us.

For years, the voice of resignation has whispered in our ears. If we listen carefully, we can still hear its echo anytime we begin courting our dreams. Bound to the same fate as Shakespearian kings, we had lethal poison poured in our ears while we were sleeping. We are served our dose of subliminal depressants from the time we are infants: a flow of concrete on the buds of our destiny. It is not a direct attack, but a constant buzzing that works on us from within. Settle for realistic goals. Lower your expectations. Be practical. Why don't you do as everyone else does? Anything that goes up must come down. Don't ask for too much. Don't go beyond the limits. Don't fly too high. Humility. Moderation. Acceptance. Don't risk. Don't experiment. Uncharted territories are dangerous. You have no experience, just dreams. This is only a utopia, but the Real World is different. Do you think you are that special? You can't make it. You are just an idealist. We are simple, imperfect human beings and must be satisfied with our lot. Certain things only happen in fairytales, real life is something else.

More or less explicitly, we hear these messages from various sources almost every day of our lives. Any attempt to experiment with different lifestyles meets with ridicule and contempt. They tell us that following the Call inviting us to live out our dreams means a hard life, great deprivations, and—as if these were not enough—almost no chances of success. We hear that chasing ideals and utopias is the pastime of lunatics with no sense of reality, rare individuals who pay with huge sacrifices and by living aloof, cut off from the Real World. In the best case, they are nice but irresponsible dreamers who, not knowing when it is time to grow up, keep playing, pretending to be heroes. They also tell us that the only true heroism is that of the hard worker who provides economic stability for the family. The true hero is the one who doesn't get lost in fantasies, but conforms to reality, setting for himself modest goals that, after years of effort, can guarantee the security and the serenity of a normal life.

Bullshit. Colossal, immense, unbelievable bullshit. There is nothing heroic in the acceptance of a sick concept of normality. If the reality surrounding you tells you to devote yourself to a dull job and embrace a life without surprises, it is neither noble nor wise to make an effort to conform. Becoming part of a system that feeds disharmony and does nothing to change the state of things is not a sign of moderation, but of mediocrity. Let's not settle for such a pathetically low ideal.

A leader is first and foremost the leader of oneself. The refusal to become part of the disease and the desire to be truly alive are what make us special and different. The Cops of Normality consider irresponsible riding one's dreams, but I think that nobody is more responsible than those who venture out searching for better ways of living. There is no great sense of responsibility in remaining attached to the material securities provided by unhappy lifestyles. Copying someone else's mistakes for fear of making bigger ones is neither courageous nor responsible, but just cowardly. The title of a book by Indian mystic Osho Rajneesh reads "Be Realistic, Plan for a Miracle." True responsibility lies in following wonderful paradoxes like this one. Answering the Call is not an extreme sacrifice, since we are sacrificing nothing truly meaningful. It can be frightening to go beyond the boundaries traced by society and to move into uncharted territory, putting at risk economic security and social reputation. But if we choose not to risk, we end up paying a much higher price. The only true sacrifice is not answering the Call, because only out there, beyond the boundaries in which we limit ourselves, can we find better ways of living.

It takes individuals with indomitable spirits to evade the negative conditioning caging us. Nice people don't stand a chance in this game. Gentle souls with good intentions lack the power to have any significant impact. Only warriors with sacred fire in their eyes possess the will to get back on their feet after being knocked down time and time again. It is at this point that martial arts come into play. Hidden between the fighting techniques are the tools to forge our character. As a sculptor creates a masterpiece starting from crude stone, martial artists can extract spiritual warriors from their personalities. The traits that are necessary to challenge our limits and be unafraid of battle are precisely those that can be developed through martial arts. More than an end in itself, martial arts practice can serve as the training ground to prepare us for the real game.

But let's try to take it a step further. The bodhisatva is one of the most beautiful figures of the Buddhist pantheon. Different from those who, after reaching enlightenment, ascend to superior realms of existence leaving behind the material world, the bodhisatva comes back to Earth using his/her power for the benefit of all living beings. The bodhisatva doesn't have all the answers and is not a raving messiah claiming to save the world. He is a calm warrior, aware of his powers, and ready to use them. Some American Indian tribes have a similar idea. They say that it is a warrior's duty to take care of everything and everybody. Just as the bodhisatvas have achieved an awareness allowing them things out of the ordinary, warriors have the strength to do what others cannot. Thus it is their responsibility to share their talent.

Having the power of a force of nature doesn't help, if you don't know what to use it for. Stealing from the gods the fire of passion and creativity to lighten our life is just the first step of the trip, not the destination. Passion and creativity are not our private property, nor our very own toys. They are the sparks lighting the fire of a big tribal camp. Having talent and not cultivating it is a crime, but cultivating it without sharing its fruits with others may be even worse. In its highest form, the way of the warrior is that of the bodhisatva: putting one's talent at the service of a superior destiny.

Forging spirit and character can take years, but it is only the preparation before the real battle. Many people train and prepare by walking along the way of the warrior, but never discover, or maybe just forget, what battle they have been training for. The battle rages in front of their eyes and they don't even realize it. The small psychodramas of daily life distract them to the point of taking away their global vision and making them forget why they set out walking along the warrior's path in the first place.

The battle is against mental limits, dullness, short-sightedness. It is against resignation, greed, sadness. Against all those powers that separate human beings from happiness. The warrior doesn't walk into battle only for himself. The warrior fights for everything and everyone. He views the destiny of the entire planet as a personal matter. As a warrior, you are given weapons very few people possess. The self-confidence of a wild animal, a spirit that can't be broken, the tranquillity of one whose roots are too deep to be disturbed by minor events. If you don't change the world, certainly nobody else will. Changing the world has nothing to do with altruism or with trying to be a good Samaritan. Ultimately, since everything is connected, helping others inevitably means helping ourselves. At the highest level, there is no difference between egoism and altruism. It is a karmic ping-pong game. All our actions come back to us.

But it is easier to convert the Abominable Snowman to surfing than finding people who dare to dream big. I am allergic to people who start talking by saying "I just want to do my own little thing … " and I sneeze often because they are everywhere. Every one of us knows some of them. Maybe they are smart, and maybe they have talent, but they have a problem. They are small. They think small. They act small. They dream small. They are what happens to people when a green-thumbed God tries to create human-bonsai. You might think that a team of Japanese engineers specialized in miniaturization were commissioned to work on their ambitions. They are the pygmies of the soul. Fans of minimalism. Armchair artists, new-agers, players who, when the game heats up, are afraid of taking in their hands the ball deciding the fate of the game, failed businessmen who recycled themselves into reiki masters (sorry, if the last example doesn't fit well, but I just felt like picking on reiki masters.) Too fearful to wholeheartedly follow their visions, they accept becoming the shadows of what they could have been.

Even some of the best people I know live by the "I just wanna do my own little thing." Satisfied with the happy little island they created for themselves in the middle of the ocean of the surrounding disharmony, they look at life from their seat in the audience. I have so many friends who have chosen to live this way that it doesn't shock me anymore. Nonetheless, I still consider this attitude one of the main causes of the mediocrity in the state of things. Often for creative people the beauty of their inner world can become a handicap. Too caught up by their subjective experience to learn how to dance through the physical world. The result is that, limiting themselves to the cultivation of their own spiritual world, the most sensitive people leave to the most careless the management of collective reality. Pragmatists without horizons, or dreamers cut off from the Real World. This dichotomy is both masochistic and dangerous. Accepting it equates a spiritual hara-kiri.

Only a surfer of emotions can mend this fracture which tears apart the potential of individuals as well as the health of the planet. Somebody able to ride in balance between the waves of yin and yang. A poet warrior. A hippie samurai. The last image is not just a metaphor, but is the root of the kind of human being who could rewrite the rules of the game. Stereotypes blackmail us and try to convince us that we can only be one thing: either pragmatists or visionaries, either romantics or realists, either artists or athletes. If we buy into this idea and fall into the trap of clearly defined roles, we end up settling for a very low definition of what we can be. Specialists without global vision. Fractions of the happy divinities we forget to be.

On the contrary, the hippie samurai is the perfect Tao. It is a sweet samurai who smiles and dances softly under the moonlight.

It is a reliable, organized hippie who arrives on time to any appointment and has the lucidity to manage an economic empire. The hippie samurai is what the yin and the yang talk about over dinner. It is the synthesis between sensitivity and efficiency. A recipe of mystic sensuality and Zen muscles. Am I kidding? Am I letting the lyricism of paradoxes lead me astray? Not at all. The hippie samurai is the union of two archetypes that shouldn't sound new to martial artists. An artist and a warrior: a martial artist. A hippie who ignores the code of honor and the warrior power of a samurai is prisoner of his own limits, just as much as a samurai who doesn't know how to relax, how to joke, how to play with children, or how to lose himself in laughter as he plays the banjo under the stars. One without the other is a caricature at best. In facing the complexity of the modern world, the stereotypes of the spaced-out, artistic hippie and of the belligerent samurai living only to fight anyone crossing his road would be at best anachronistic, and in the worst case, just pathetic. Throughout the world, the resurrection of the warrior's spirit is badly needed, but the solution cannot come from blindly copying old models. Being warriors today is more difficult than ever because there is no ready-made formula that we can follow to stand up to the increasing complexity of our time.

What we need is a new alchemy. The new warrior can only be born from a hazardous synthesis, from unlikely marriages such as the one between hippie and samurai. It is not a question of going to battle against The Enemy, a kind of ultimate villain who, in the style of James Bond movies, oppresses the whole world. If it were so, it would be easy, but reality is much more complicated. Shallowness and mediocrity kill more people than the most ruthless tyranny. Being warriors today is about fighting those forces trying to crush us as much as it is about having powerful visions. Creating new ways of life is the way to give battle. The challenge is not about destroying something or someone. It is about creating. A warrior is a master at facing conflicts, and conflict is what stands between us and the fulfillment of our desires. But to ransom oneself and the world from the wretchedness of a depressed way of life, the warrior has to do more than fight any specific circumstance.

To be able to touch the heart of the problem, we need the imagination to reinvent the world. The Enemy that keeps us prisoners is not an individual, a political party, or a religion (even though individuals, political parties and some religions certainly contribute); rather the entire social structure we have created is the problem. Maybe, at an even deeper level, it is our way of viewing life: the necessity of an authentic spirituality, our relationship with the natural world, the way we use technology, the jobs we devote so much of our time to, the houses in which we live, the friendships we cultivate. These are the places where the battle is fought. A boundless heart, the gift of synthesis and far-reaching eyes are our weapons.

We started chatting about martial arts and we ended up with the destiny of the world in our hands. We didn't arrive at this point because we got lost on the way but because, if we truly follow the spirit of martial arts, it is inevitable to find ourselves here. "The Way of a Warrior is to establish harmony," wrote Ueshiba. Martial arts are the bow and the arrow. The target is the creation of harmony outside of us and within us. There are many other means to hit the target, for being warriors is essentially a state of mind. One can be a warrior in hundreds of different way. Martial arts are a beautiful path to forge those qualities we need for any great undertaking, but they are by no means the only one. If we want to have a chance to succeed at recreating the world around us, we can't let differences divide us. We owe it to life, to the earth and to ourselves. If we don't do it, who else will?

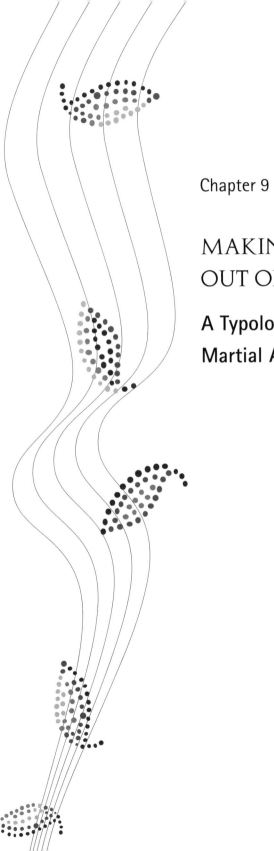

Chapter 9

MAKING ORDER
OUT OF CHAOS

A Typology of
Martial Arts Styles

To those faithful readers who have made it this far, my deepest thanks for sharing with me several hours of your life. Precisely because you have been such graceful companions, I feel I owe you an apology for what I'm about to do. The chapter you are about to read, in fact, is nothing like the rest of this book. If you have had fun with me so far, this chapter may make you change your mind. Here, you'll find that my writing style is unaccounted for. Some reports state that it has been spotted lazily sipping tequila on a Mexican beach. Others say that too many hours in graduate school being interrogated by the academic secret police has driven it into a deep depression, and it is now wandering the UCLA campus mumbling incoherent words (if found, please, please, please be kind and return it to its legitimate owner. A reward is available. I miss it very much!) Equally missing is any attempt to connect martial arts to a wider context. This chapter begins with martial arts, continues with martial arts, and ends with martial arts. References to any other part of life—which fill the rest of the book— find in this chapter as much sympathy as a country musician can find in Harlem. I could continue the list of what is missing from this chapter for quite a while, but the hour is late and I'm afraid it is time for me to begin telling you what this chapter _is_ indeed about and why I want to include it despite its deficiencies.

After countless discussions, I have come to realize that most non-martial artists have some bizarre notions regarding the nature of different types of martial arts. More surprising, however, has been running into thousands of martial artists and realizing that many of them have similarly cloudy ideas. This is where this chapter comes in. Intended as an antidote to the general confusion many people have about martial arts styles, it seeks to provide an analytical blueprint for understanding the roots of different arts. For the sake of clarity, I selected a simple, unadorned, "to the point" kind of writing style to take care of the job. Faced with the happy prospect of getting paid to teach a series of courses at UCLA about the history, philosophy and practice of Asian martial arts, I wrote this chapter in an effort to help my students develop a better understanding of the world of martial arts as a whole. It is my hope that this work may help you too. If it doesn't, I renew my apologies and suggest that you simply flip the pages and skip to the next one.

INTRODUCTION

Judo, Aikido, Karate, and Kendo. Shaolin, *Wing Chun,* White Crane, *and Hung Gar. Silat,* Kali, *Choy Li Fut,* and *Tae Kwon Do. Iaido, Sambo, Hapkido,* and *Hwarang Do.* And then Western Boxing, Greco-Roman Wrestling, Freestyle Wrestling, Shuai Chiao, Jujitsu, Tai Chi Chuan, Pa Kua, Hsing-i, Muay Thai, Kenjutsu, *Kyudo, Savate, Kuntao,* Sumo, *I-Chuan,* Drunken Boxing, *Kobudo.* This martial rap has barely scratched the surface of the names of all the martial arts styles in existence. A quick glance at the martial arts section in your local Yellow Pages is enough to bring us in contact with the astonishing variety of martial arts forms. To the uninitiated (and often to the initiated too), such variety is overwhelming and confusing. Don't most human beings have two legs and two arms? Why are there so many different schools to teach how to beat up another human opponent? What is it that separates one style from the next? Is one style better than another? What makes them different?

Vast numbers of martial artists have never asked themselves these questions or, if they have, swallowed simplistic, self-serving answers offered by their teachers (usually sounding something like, "We train like this because it's the best way, they train differently because they don't know any better") and never inquired further. With their curiosity satisfied, these martial artists go on practicing their style of choice knowing preciously little about the theory and history behind their art, and knowing next to nothing about other styles' histories and training methods. Go to any school, ask a few questions and it should quickly become clear that ignorance of other styles is the norm among martial artists.

The present chapter is an attempt to clarify what the boundaries between the different styles stand for. In time I have run across many analytical models grouping martial arts styles in categories based on geographic origin, and/or physical characteristics, and/or philosophical orientation, as well as several other variables. (For a summary of some of the most famous models, see Donohue 1994) Although all of these models are the result of a sincere effort to grope for clarity in the midst of the chaotic world of martial arts, they did not prove to be completely satisfactory to me. For this reason, I ended up coming up with my own model, which I will outline in the following pages. My purpose here is twofold. First, I want to provide a tool to help martial artists wishing to better see how a certain style relates to all others. Second, I offer this model to prospective martial artists so that they can make more educated decisions about picking an art that fits their needs. In other words, the model should help answer questions such as what does training in a certain art entail? What aspects do different arts emphasize? What can one expect from training in one art rather than another?

The model I present here divides martial arts styles into a few simple categories based on two criteria: which goals do certain arts emphasize, and which training methods do they favor. This is not The Perfect Model, but is just one possible model. It has worked well for me and helped me better understand martial arts. I hope it can do the same for you.

THE MODEL

According to this model, all martial arts styles can be divided in the following five categories:

1. Performance Arts
2. Internal Arts
3. Weapons Arts
4. Self Defense Arts
5. Combat Sports
    Grappling
    Striking
    Combined

Before I move on to explain what these categories mean, let me warn you that these categories are not mutually exclusive. Rather, most styles may belong to several categories at once, but in most cases they tend to place their emphasis mainly on one of these five aspects.

PERFORMANCE ARTS

Performance Arts are those martial styles that focus the majority of their attention on the aesthetic appeal of the art. In these styles, the training in realistic combat techniques is a secondary component, if it is a component at all. Rather, the bulk of training revolves around performing martial-looking movements in the most beautiful way possible. Instead of being fighting styles in the purest sense of the word, Performance Arts combine gymnastics and martial arts movements, resulting in what is better termed as a "martial dance." The styles belonging to this category are usually spectacular and flashy, require excellent athletic abilities, and are highly unrealistic with regard to fighting. Precisely because of these characteristics, they are ideal choices when it comes to portraying martial arts in movies, since choreographers choose martial techniques not for their effectiveness but for their spectacular effect on the screen.

Modern Wushu, a Chinese martial art developed in the twentieth century from the roots of what used to be combat-oriented styles, is perhaps the best example what of a Performance Art is. Whereas all traditional styles of Chinese martial arts have students train in forms (codified sequences of techniques to be executed in the air, without a live opponent) along with other training methods, Modern Wushu focuses almost exclusively on improving the aesthetic dimension of forms. Training in Wushu means first and foremost training for the sake of beauty.

Since historically martial arts schools had been a fertile ground for rebel groups combining martial training with opposition to the central government, the Communist government that has ruled over

China since the 1950s tried to prevent the formation of a combat-trained opposition within the country. For this reason, as well as for its opposition to all vestiges of "old" culture, it made it a policy of persecuting traditional combat-oriented Kung Fu schools. As part of the repression against the fighting arts, the Communist government also encouraged the transition from combat styles to the state-sponsored, less threatening, performance-oriented Modern Wushu. Many other Kung Fu styles followed suit, and although they may retain the names of older fighting arts, they have similarly switched their attention almost completely to form-training (which may include hand-forms, forms with weapons, and two-person forms which are prearranged fighting sequences). For this reason, most Chinese martial arts in modern times belong to the category of Performance Arts (Miller 1994).

Another style that may fit the definition of Performance Art is *Capoeira*. Originated in Brazil among the African slaves, Capoeira is always performed to the sound of music. The reason for this—according to a popular theory—is that practitioners of Capoeira trained in fighting techniques, but in order to avoid the unwanted attention of the slave-masters, who probably would have not approved, disguised their training as a form of dance. For this reason, Capoeira looks like a martial dance combining kicks and acrobatic movements to the sound of the *berimbau* and other Brazilian instruments. In more recent times, although it is still possible to find Capoeiristas who know how to use their art to fight, the emphasis in most Capoeira schools has shifted away from stressing the effectiveness of the fighting techniques, and moved more toward making Capoeira a beautiful dance to watch and practice (Almeida 1986, Capoeira 1995).

Both Capoeira and Modern Wushu show how combat-oriented arts (which is what all martial arts were at some point) can turn into something else once the cultural and historical context changes. Even though Capoeira, Modern Wushu and most types of Kung Fu are the styles that better fit the description of Performance Arts, some emphasis on aesthetic performance is present in several other styles—from Tai Chi Chuan to certain forms of Karate—that train at least to some degree with the goal of "looking good" in mind.

INTERNAL ARTS

Often, in many martial arts circles—in particular among the practitioners of Tai Chi Chuan, Hsing-i, Pa Kua, and Aikido—some fighting styles are classified as "Internal" as opposed to all the other "External" styles. Although the reality of this classification is debatable, these terms have become popular enough that they deserve some attention.

According to the popular theory, so-called internal styles rely on the development of Chi power obtained thanks to breathing and balancing exercises as well as standing and sitting meditation. External styles, on the other hand, rely on more visible forms of power dependent on brute strength and superior speed. When one moves beyond the somewhat complicated task of explaining exactly what qi power is supposed to be, the principles of the Internal Arts are nothing different from the principles of any good fighting style. The ideas of exploiting the opponent's weakness, of not opposing force against a superior force, of relying on proper technique and good body dynamics more than on muscular strength, have as much to do with Internal Arts as they do with common sense (Cartmell 1997). The Japanese arts of Judo and Jujitsu, for example, which are rarely ever classified as internal, are based on the same theory (Kano 1986, Kirby 1983). Therefore, other than more emphasis on the somewhat nebulous field of Chi development, one is hard pressed to find a theoretical difference separating Internal Arts from all other fighting styles.

Another complication arises from the historical origin of Internal Arts. Until the period around the end of the nineteenth and the beginning of the twentieth century, in fact, no martial style had ever been identified as an "Internal" Art. It was only when Pa Kua master Cheng Ting Hua formed an alliance with teachers of Hsing-i and Tai Chi Chuan that they began to use the word "internal" to refer to their styles. In particular it was one of Cheng Ting Hua's most famous students, Sun Lu Tang, who publicized this classification in a series of popular books (Henning 1997, Sun 1993). A few decades later, some people similarly classified the Japanese art of Aikido as "internal," since its particular emphasis on *Ki* (the Japanese spelling for Chi) development and its philosophical orientation were thought to make the style closer to the Chinese Internal Arts than to the old Jujitsu schools.

Regardless of the fact that neither theory nor history seems to offer much ground for the classification of some arts as "Internal," in modern times genuine differences in goals and training methods seem to exist between so-called Internal Styles and all other martial arts. In a perfect self-fulfilling prophecy, after repeating long enough that styles such as Tai Chi Chuan, Pa Kua, Hsing-i, and Aikido were different from all others, their practice and orientation have been changed in a way that now they *are* indeed different. Although these arts were originally created as efficient combat forms (one only has to think about the reputation of tremendous fighters such as Aikido's Ueshiba, Pa Kua's Cheng Ting Hua, Hsing-i's Kuo Yun Shen, and Tai Chi Chuan's Yang Lu Chan), in recent times these arts are rarely taught with the goal of fighting in mind. Rather, the focus has shifted to health maintenance, meditation, philosophy, and body-awareness. One just has to picture the familiar sightings of old ladies slowly performing the movements of the Taiji form to notice how far some of these arts are now removed from the realm of combat.

In most schools, the bulk of training in the arts of Tai Chi Chuan, Pa Kua, and Hsing-i consists of breathing exercises, other Chi Kung exercises for balance and flexibility, standing meditation, and most importantly the practice of forms performed with the goal of improving the practitioner's health and physical condition. Less often, some of these schools include the practice of push-hands (an exercise designed to increase the practitioner's sensitivity), weapon forms, and some fighting techniques performed with a partner. Only in those very rare schools that still teach these styles as viable combat arts, is competitive training such as full-contact sparring practiced. In the vast majority of schools, however, the time dedicated to self-defense techniques is very limited, and sparring is nonexistent.

In a similar fashion, training in the art of Aikido does not include sparring and other competitive combat games. Rather, the practice is centered on basic exercises (including the art of rolling and falling), and techniques practiced with a cooperative partner. In some cases, form training with weapons is included, but is rarely emphasized. It is important to note that in most Aikido schools, like in the schools of Chinese Internal Arts, the techniques are not drilled with the goal of effective self-defense in mind, but to teach awareness of one's own energy as well as of someone else's energy. Clear evidence of this is the fact that powerful fighting tools such as headbutts, elbow strikes, knee strikes, eye-gouging, chokes, ground-fighting, and kicks are rarely ever taught.

The reasons for the drastic changes that these arts have gone through from their origin to their present form are somewhat complicated. In regards to the Chinese arts, the Chinese tradition of secrecy and the reluctance of many masters to share their full-knowledge of fighting with their students has caused much of the combat-training to die out without being passed down the generations. Another factor is the advent of the Communist regime and its repressive policies against the practice of effective fighting arts. Under Communist rule, Chinese martial arts were transformed from combat styles into Performance Arts and Internal Arts concerned with goals that the government perceived as desirable such as physical fitness and health maintenance (Miller 1994).

In the case of Aikido, the transformation is in part due to the character of Aikido's founder Morihei Ueshiba. A mystically inclined man heavily influenced by the Omoto religious sect, Ueshiba was deeply disturbed by World War II, and after the war proceeded to reduce the stress he placed on combat training and to increase the importance of energy-awareness and philosophy. In Ueshiba's mind, Aikido was to become a physical vehicle for peace and for the establishment of good relations between human beings rather than a method of fighting. It was this change in Ueshiba's approach which prompted Aikido to move further from the Jujitsu schools in which it originated and establish itself as a very different kind of martial art (Stevens 1987, Ueshiba 1984, Ueshiba 1991).

Because of this change in orientation, arts like Aikido, Tai Chi Chuan, Hsing-i, and Pa Kua have attracted and continue to attract very peculiar kind of customers: new-agers, pacifists who wouldn't want to have anything to do with brutal fighting arts, older people concerned with health maintenance, and philosophically-inclined individuals are now the main clients of Internal Arts schools (as well as being the most prolific readers of books about martial arts). Although it is true that this fact has caused these styles to become virtually extinct as viable forms of combat training, it does not mean that these arts are only watered-down relics of what they once were. Simply, the goals have changed. The attempt to instill in its practitioners a more balanced personality, and the health benefits of lower blood pressure, better balance, reduced stress levels, and better posture enjoyed by the practitioners of these arts are certainly not something that should be easily dismissed. Internal Arts may not be anymore the ideal choice for those looking for an effective fighting style, but they nonetheless occupy an important niche in the world of modern martial arts.

WEAPONS ARTS

As the name indicates, Weapons Arts are those martial arts in which training with weapons takes the primary role. In more ancient times, almost all martial arts were Weapons Arts since the majority of fighting styles were concerned with survival on the battlefield, or with self-defense in a world where most people carried on them some kind of weapons. Only in those times and places in which carrying weapons was illegal, would hand-to-hand combat take center stage. Otherwise, no one in their right mind would rely on empty-hand tactics if weapons were available. Contrary to what happens in our times, hand-to-hand combat was a smaller sub-field of martial systems that focused most of their attention on weapons training (Draeger 1973).

In our times, the picture is drastically reversed. With the exception of soldiers who still practice with weapons much more than they do without, the majority of martial arts training takes place among civilians who are not concerned with survival on a battlefield. Also, the fact that in many nations several restrictions are placed on the possession of weapons, combined with the possibly severe legal repercussions of using a weapon even in cases of self-defense, has contributed to shifting the focus of martial arts practice from training with weapons to hand-to-hand training.

Despite this drastic change, many fighting styles still include training with weapons as a secondary component of their curriculum. The majority of Kung Fu styles (including the Performance Art of Modern Wushu), several Korean arts, Aikido, and some schools of Jujitsu all dedicate some fractions of time to weapons training. However, despite some notable exceptions, the quality of instruction and expertise shown in handling weapons is often shamefully low. Without an outlet as a combat sport and removed from the sphere of realistic self-defense (when was the last time that you had to fight a horse-riding, spear-wielding drunken neighbor with your favorite halberd?), weapons training is usually taught only for its symbolic appeal. Realistic techniques have often been long lost and in their place are taught weapons forms chosen for their aesthetic beauty. In the majority of cases, when actual techniques are taught, they rarely meet the definition of effective.

There are still other arts, however, that are dedicated either primarily or even exclusively to the practice with weapons. Western fencing—a modern competitive version of the sword-skills once used by European fighters—and the Okinawan art of Kobudo—a style based on the techniques and farming tools employed by the indigenous population after the Japanese invaders prohibited the ownership of conventional weapons—are two of the most famous weapons-based arts. The Japanese arts of Kendo, Iaido and Kyudo are perfect examples of modern Weapons Arts adapted from the older styles of sword-fighting and archery practiced in former times by the Japanese samurai.

Kendo, the way of the sword, is a modern sportive version of Japanese fencing that requires practicing techniques and sparring with a live opponent while clad in protective armor and armed with a bamboo sword. Iaido is another sword-based art, but unlike Kendo does not feature sparring with an opponent. Rather, it focuses on the practice of katas designed to teach the skills once used by the samurai to extract the sword from the scabbard and execute a potentially deadly technique in as little time as possible (Draeger and Smith 1969). Kyudo, on the other hand, is the modern version of Japanese archery, which still uses the traditional long bow and is often practiced as a complement to the study of Zen philosophy (Herrigel 1953).

Among the several other martial arts that still dedicate substantial time and attention to weapons training are the nearly unknown Indian art of Kalarippayattu, the Japanese art of Ninjutsu, as well as several Southeast Asian martial arts (Draeger and Smith 1969). The most popular of them is perhaps the Filipino art known as Kali (aka Escrima). Although Kali includes empty-hand training, it is most famous for its use of short weapons, in particular short sword and dagger, single and double sticks, and knives of various sizes and shapes. Contrary to most other Weapons Arts, which are now completely anachronistic from the point of view of realistic combat training since swords, spears, halberds, bows and arrows are not commonly used anymore, Kali can still teach practical skills. In fact, short sticks, clubs and knives are—with the exception of guns—some of the most useful self-defense tools in the modern world. For this reason, the applicability and realism of the techniques taught is stressed in Kali much more than in other Weapons Arts. In order to accomplish this goal, Kali training is based both on the practice of techniques with a cooperative partner as well as on full-contact sparring with protective equipment (Inosanto 1980). With the exception of Kali, most other Weapons Arts are practiced with goals other than realistic combat training in mind. The appeals of the arts include different aims such as aesthetic performance, cultural significance, transmission of ethnic heritage, and sport competition.

SELF-DEFENSE ARTS

Simply stated, Self-Defense Arts are those arts that are primarily concerned with imparting combat skills designed to work in a real fight. Although the definition may seem straightforward, it is not. In fact, Combat Sports (those disciplines teaching how to fight in a sportive dimension bound by many rules limiting the range of possible techniques) often teach excellent skills that can be used in a self-defense situation. However, the main purpose of these arts is to teach practitioners how to fight within the confines a sport event. Pure Self-Defense Arts, on the other hand, place a secondary importance on training for tournaments (if they place any importance on it at all) and instead focus on preparing for defense against assaults on the street.

Among some of the most clearly identifiable Self Defense Arts are most schools of Japanese Jujitsu, Chinese styles such as Wing Chun and Kung Fu San Soo (aka Tsoi Li Ho Fut Hung), Indonesian Silat, Bruce Lee's Jeet Kune Do, Korean Hapkido, and perhaps Hwarang-do. Several other styles of Kung Fu, Aikido, and Karate also claim to belong to this category, but one should be cautious at evaluating how successful they are at this, since there is tremendous variety in the quality of the training methods employed by those claiming to teach good self-defense.

Since Self-Defense Arts teach to use potentially devastating techniques that attack all targets and are not restricted by any rules, one question begs an answer. How can they accomplish this result while simultaneously ensuring the safety of their students? Since training these techniques in a no-rules format would imply extreme physical damage, by necessity Self-Defense Arts employ other tactics. Among the most common training methods are the practice of specific techniques executed with restraint on a cooperative opponent, two-person forms which take the students through a prearranged sequence of attack and defense, a spontaneous free-flow format in which a student combines techniques on the spot to defend against the attacks of a cooperative opponent, and occasionally some type of limited rule-bound sparring like the kind employed by Combat Sports (Cartmell 1997).

Each of these forms of training has its advantages and disadvantages, but combined together they are supposed to help practitioners develop the necessary tools for self-defense without the physical damage that engaging in real fights would entail. Potentially deadly techniques, in fact, cannot safely be practiced against an uncooperative opponent because it is very easy to take them too far and seriously injure one's training partners. For this reason, techniques are first practiced with a cooperative training partner who allows one to use his/her body to get the technique right.

This, of course, is a basic method in any Self-Defense Art, without which any further learning would be impossible. However, it presents obvious limitations. First, our partner is fully cooperating with us and, in effect, is letting us execute a technique, which may or may not work when done at full-speed against an uncooperative opponent. For this reason, it is hard to know whether the very same technique would work for real or not. Furthermore, since this kind of training is not spontaneous, it does not help solving one of the main problems people encounter in a real fight: freezing while trying to remember which technique to apply and thus being unable to adapt to the present situation. After all, in this context we know ahead of time in which way our training partner will attack us and we know how we are going to respond. This is completely unlike reality, where we do not know what attack will come and therefore also do not know how we will respond. Just because one knows how to execute a technique within a school does not mean that he or she will be able to remember and apply that technique at the right moment, while adrenaline is flowing, against an unexpected attack.

Two-person forms have the additional advantage of combining

a sequence of techniques together but the same problems apply: the techniques are prearranged and our training partner is not resisting.

Once enough basic techniques are mastered, the spontaneous free-flow format in which one responds with an unplanned technique to defend against the unexpected attacks of a cooperative opponent is the necessary next step. Unfortunately, this type of training is not as common as one would expect. Kung Fu San Soo is one of the few styles that—to my knowledge—utilizes this format for most of its training. This format has the tremendous advantage of making the application of techniques spontaneous and immediate without having to stop to think about them. Since the opponent is cooperative and is offering only minimal resistance, all kinds of techniques—including potentially lethal ones, used against all kind of targets—can be practiced. The downfall is that precisely because the opponent is not really an opponent who is fighting back but a cooperative training partner, again there is no way to know if these techniques would work against an aggressor fully determined to hurt us.

Since most Self-Defense Arts base their training on the methods outlined above, even though they are technically more complete than Combat Sports they are sometimes less effective. In fact, whereas one never knows if these methods would work against an uncooperative opponent, successfully applying a technique in the course of a full-contact sparring match against an opponent who is trying to defend him/herself and attack us back offers concrete proof of perfect timing and power. This indicates that these two approaches should not be alternative to each other (Combat Sport training, as we will soon see, has its own disadvantages), but should be complementary. Since there is no substitute for reality, all methods that simulate real conditions while maintaining safety should be employed in order for training to be as effective as possible. In fact, each form of training in martial arts is a distant approximation of reality and for this reason each has weaknesses and strengths.

Several Self-Defense systems actually combine these different forms of training, but the results are not always ideal. In most cases, Self-Defense Arts devote the majority of their attention to specific techniques, forms and perhaps to free-flow cooperative training. If they move on to sparring, however, since they do not give to this facet of training as much attention as do Combat Sports, they are far inferior to them. The case of Kung Fu schools practicing beautiful forms and extremely sophisticated techniques only to put the gloves on and engage in a particularly inept kind of kickboxing is very common. This is not to say that these combinations between "pure" self-defense training and combat games are not possible— many schools do it very well—but the perfect balance is not as common as we could wish.

COMBAT SPORTS

Combat Sports are those martial arts that focus their practice on some forms of sparring. The focus in these arts is the participation in sporting events. The philosophical side of martial arts, self-defense training, health maintenance and other factors that are important in other martial arts are secondary elements of training (if they are elements at all.) Combat Sports athletes train to participate in tournaments to test their sparring skills. As indicated earlier, sparring has the disadvantage of employing a limited range of techniques against a limited number of targets (some of the most effective targets for the purpose of self-defense being prohibited for safety reasons.) But it also offers the invaluable experience of applying techniques full power against someone who is fighting back, which is precisely what would happen in reality.

In ancient Greece, Combat Sports were the highlight of the Olympic Games. At that time, three kind of Combat Sports were practiced: Boxing, Wrestling, and Pankration, depending on whether the competition focused on grappling (Wrestling), striking (Boxing), or a combination of the two (Pankration) (Poliakoff, 1987). Since many modern Combat Sports still follow the same division, here I'll examine these three different kinds of Combat Sports separately.

Grappling

Grappling systems are those Combat Sports that focus on throws and takedowns, and/or on groundfighting (which depending on the system includes pins and/or chokes and/or leverages.) Examples of these arts are Kodokan Judo, Sumo, Brazilian Jujitsu, Chinese Shuai Chiao, Russsian Sambo, and the Western systems of Greco-Roman and Freestyle Wrestling. In addition to these systems, there are many forms of ethnic wrestling (from Mongolia to Africa, just about every country in the world has some form of wrestling) and eclectic systems based on some of the most popular grappling arts outlined above.

The differences between these arts have to do with the rules they abide by. The most important difference is whether a system is exclusively dedicated to takedowns and throws but does not include groundfighting (like Sumo, Shuai Chiao, and Mongolian Wrestling), or it employs both (like Judo, Brazilian Jujitsu, Sambo, and Western Wrestling.) In the first group, the winner is the athlete who can execute a perfect throw while maintaining his/her own balance. In the second group, depending on the system, one may win because of a perfect throw, because of pinning the opponent to the floor, or because of a submission (choke or leverage) on the ground.

Another important difference has to do with the amount of clothing worn by the athletes in competition (since clothing can be grabbed to make throws easier, the kind of throws employed change depending on the uniform worn.) Here is a breakdown of the main characteristics of some of these styles.

Judo: Judo players wear a heavy jacket called a gi which is grabbed to execute the throws and facilitate submissions on the ground. Most of the throws are hip throws, hand throws, sweeps, and sacrifice throws (those throws in which one willingly goes to the ground in order to take down the opponent). Judo discourages grabbing the opponent's legs (a common technique in Freestyle Wrestling) to execute a throw. On the ground, Judo players aim at pinning the opponent with his back on the floor, or choking him in a variety of ways, or applying a leverage (the only leverages allowed are against the elbow joint). (Kano 1986, Takagaki 1957)

Sumo: Sumo players rely on takedowns and throws. Pushing the opponent out of the circle delimitating the ring or taking him to the ground are the ways to achieve victory. Hardly any clothing is worn during the matches and no leverages or chokes are allowed.

Brazilian Jujitsu: This recent form of Jujitsu (created in the twentieth century) specializes in groundfighting. Fighters wear a Judo gi. Matches begin standing up but quickly a takedown (usually a simpler, less flashy kind than those seen in Judo) takes the match to the ground where chokes and leverages are applied. Legal leverages are those against almost any joint other than the fingers.

Shuai Chiao: Shuai Chiao fighters wear a light jacket (much lighter than in Judo.) For this reason, since they lack enough cloth to pull as much as Judo players do, they have to come closer to each other. Shuai Jiao does not include groundfighting, but focuses exclusively on powerful throws and takedowns which often involve joint-locking (Liang 1997, Weng 1984).

Sambo: Sambo is an eclectic system combining Judo, Greco-Roman, and Freestyle Wrestling with ethnic forms of Russian Wrestling. Players wear a light jacket, and rely on throws as well as on groundfighting. On the ground, chokes are not allowed but leverages against most joints (including ankle and knee) are (Anderson & B 1999).

Western Wrestling: Western Wrestlers wear light uniforms that cannot be easily grabbed to execute throws. For this reason,

Western Wrestling favors either grabbing the legs to score a takedown or powerful body lifts resulting in a throw. On the ground, Wrestlers aim at pinning the opponent but cannot apply chokes or joint-locks. The main difference between Greco-Roman and Freestyle Wrestling is that Greco-Roman does not allow attacking the opponent's legs or using one's own legs to execute a throw whereas Freestyle does.

Among the good aspects of grappling systems from the point of view of realistic fighting is the fact that in reality it is very hard to keep an opponent at the distance required for the striking range, and clinching often follows the initial blows. For this reason, grappling systems offer the invaluable advantage of making one comfortable being at close quarters with an opponent.

Groundfighting, in particular, is an excellent form of training since contrary to stand-up fighting—where even if they are not trained, most people have some instinctive notions of what to do—it is entirely learned. For this reason as well as for the fact that often one may end up on the ground whether he/she wants it or not, a person with a little knowledge of groundfighting is far ahead of one who does not know anything about it. The disadvantage of specializing too much in groundfighting is that ending up on the ground is suicidal in a situation where one has to face multiple opponents, since while one is busy fighting one opponent his still-standing friends can stomp on his/her head.

The throwing component of grappling systems is possibly the most important part one needs to master for the sake of realistic fighting. In fact, since the vast majority of fights end up in the clinching range, if one is able to execute a throw, the chances of success sharply increase because taking a hard fall on concrete can knock out even the toughest opponents. Furthermore, in a situation with multiple opponents, one can incapacitate an opponent by throwing him hard and immediately move on to the next person or run.

One of the problems inherent in grappling training, as far as realistic fighting goes, is that some of the rules teach bad habits that would be very dangerous to follow in a real situation. For example, when Judo players and Western wrestlers turn face down while on the ground in order to avoid being pinned with their back against the floor, they are effectively exposing their head and neck to the opponent. Of course, this would be the worse thing to do in a real situation.

Striking

Striking systems are those Combat Sports that focus on one or more of the following facets of fighting: punching, kicking, striking using the elbows, and striking using the knees. Some of the most famous examples of these systems are Western Boxing, Kickboxing, Muay Thai, San Shou, Tae Kwon Do, Savate, Full-Contact Karate, and Point-Karate.

Just as in the case of the grappling systems, striking systems differ depending on which rules they follow. Also, just like the grappling systems, striking systems focus only on a particular part of combat and train it extensively for use in competition. In this sense, they are not complete martial arts systems but rather martial sports. However, they can still provide realistic combat training since they help practitioners get over the fear of opponents trying their best to attack them with full power. From the point of view of combat realism, the least amount of rules the sport has, the more useful it is. With this consideration in mind, let's examine the rules employed by some of the most famous striking sports.

Western Boxing: Boxing requires the athletes to wear heavily padded gloves and only allows striking with a specific part of the hand to most parts of the opponent's upper body (excluding the back of the neck.) Although Boxing training has many advantages, the main problem is that it creates a false sense of distance in a real combat situation (where kicks may come into play) and relies on few tools.

Muay Thai: Muay Thai allows punching and kicking as well as elbow and knee strikes to the opponent's upper and lower body (excluding the groin, which is off-limits in all striking Combat Sports, as well as a few other targets.) Because of its few restrictions, Muay Thai is one of the most punishing striking sports to practice but is also one of the most realistic.

Kickboxing: Different Kickboxing organizations adhere to different rules, but most often Kickboxing allows punching and kicking and prohibits the elbow and knee strikes employed in Muay Thai. Some Kickboxing organizations also do not allow kicks to the opponent's legs. In many cases, Full-Contact Karate tournaments follow the same rules as Kickboxing. One of the main problems with Kickboxing rules is that, because of the spectacular appeal of the technique, they invite high kicks (which are very risky in a real situation) and prohibit the less-spectacular but more effective low-kicks.

Point Karate: Although different organizations use different rules, most forms of Point-Karate require the athletes to stop the strikes short of actually hitting with power (in some cases no touching at all is allowed.) For this reason, the sport depends largely on the judges' evaluation of the techniques. This is possibly the safest of all striking sports, but is also the least realistic since it does not offer the experience of trying one's techniques with full power, and may teach a false sense of distance since one never gets to really strike the target.

San Shou: This Chinese version of Kickboxing is perhaps best characterized as a mixed system since it allows both striking and throwing, but since grappling only has a very limited role (no groundfighting, no clinching for longer than three seconds), it is primarily considered a striking system. Practitioners of all different kinds of Chinese martial arts enter San Shou (aka Sanda) competitions. San Shou allows punching and kicking to the opponent's lower and upper body, but no elbow and knee strikes. Throws are only legal if executed within three seconds of clinching with an opponent. The possibility of getting thrown helps the realism of San Shou training since it discourages high kicks that can be more easily caught by the opponent and used for a counter-throw. The lack of elbow and knee strikes makes San Shou safer than Muay Thai, but less realistic.

Tae Kwon Do: Tae Kwon Do, which is now an Olympic sport, focuses primarily on high kicks and requires practitioners to wear safety gear on their chests in addition to the standard gloves. Although it is an extremely spectacular sport, by inviting practitioners to focus on high kicks, Tae Kwon Do may instill dangerous habits since in a real combat situation high kicks often lead to loss of balance and/or a counter by the opponent.

Taken as a whole, striking systems have both weaknesses and strengths. One of the most positive aspects is the fact that most real fights begin at a long range where striking skills are very useful. Knowing how to hit with power may allow one to stop a fight at the very beginning. Also, knowing how to take a strike is equally valuable since it allows one not to freeze after getting hit (which despite claims to the contrary, can happen even to the best fighters.)

Among the negative aspects of striking systems is the fact that the human hand is not very resilient. Punches thrown in a ring while protected by heavy gloves rarely damage one's hands, but punching with bare-knuckles in a self-defense situation may cause as much damage to the person executing the technique as to the one getting hit. Whereas hitting with an open hand, or using elbows and knees is relatively safe, punching with a closed fist can easily result in a broken hand. For this reason, relying too much on punching may not be wise in a self-defense scenario.

The other, more substantial, downfall of striking systems from the point of view of combat realism is the fact that it is very hard to keep an opponent at the distance necessary for striking skills to be useful. Very often, if the initial flurry does not result in a knockout, fights end up in a clinch and in this position grappling training is more useful than striking training.

Combined Combat Sports

Just like Pankration in ancient Greece, there are several modern Combat Sports that allow both grappling and striking techniques. Chinese San Shou, although primarily a striking art, is one of these arts. In the 1990s, the world of Combat Sports was revolutionized by the popularization of no-holds-barred competitions such as the Ultimate Fighting Championship and Extreme Fighting. After these events made it clear that the best fighters are those who know both how to grapple and how to strike, many eclectic schools of martial arts have developed in order to combine both kinds of training. Some of them are Brazilian Valetudo, Shootfighting, San Shou, Combat Shuai Chiao, Sport Jujitsu and countless recently-created systems. The common thread running through all these Combined Combat Sport is the desire to escape the limitations of systems relying only on grappling or only on striking. Because of the extreme amount of training required and the potential dangers involved, practice of these Combat Sports has so far been limited to very dedicated athletes.

CONCLUSION

It is with a little bit of hesitation that I commit this model to print. One reason for my hesitation is that all models based on definitions and categories are inevitably flawed. Categories are never as rigid in reality as they are in theory. What on paper appear as rigorously separate categories may overlap in the real world. Also, I have always been suspicious of anyone worrying too much about categories and definitions. Such an analytic drive often kills the beauty of experience reducing it to a set of dead formulas. However, as long as one is aware of the limitations of any theoretical model, I believe he or she can use what follows as a pair of glasses to see better what otherwise may appear as a blurry reality.

Also, because of my personal taste and because of what I believe to be the nature of martial arts I have emphasized the importance of realistic combat training. This, however, is by no means the only criterion to judge the validity of a martial art. For this reason, depending on your personal purpose, a particular art may be better suited to your personality. A certain art may be a great vehicle for health-maintenance, but if you approach martial arts looking for a different goal, the focus on health-maintenance may disappoint you. The art is not wrong, nor are you. Simply, it is a bad match.

The picture clearly gets tricky when a particular style claims to follow several purposes at once. "Our style—a teacher may say—is great for health-maintenance, can teach amazing self-defense skills, is good for competing in tournaments, and has a strong philosophical side." The reason why this kind of claim is tricky is not that is false (although sometimes it is), but that it does not tell the whole truth. With only so much time available, all styles focus their attention on some aspects at the expense of others. Although lip-service may be paid to different goals, inevitably each school ends up specializing in one aspect more than others; therefore, prospective students need to be able to read between the lines and find out the real goals on which the school truly focuses. Each style has strengths and weaknesses. It is inevitable. For this reason, rather than looking for a utopian, perfect style which has all strengths and no weaknesses, a martial artist needs to ask him/herself whether the balance of strengths and weaknesses in a particular style fits his/her needs or not.

One more consideration to keep in mind is that martial arts are taught and learned by real flesh and blood people. A particular style may have certain defining characteristics, but the individual teachers and students can heighten or lessen them. For example, although Aikido is not known for its emphasis on self-defense, there are practitioners who train for realistic self-defense with very decent results. In the same way, Western Boxing may not be what people consider a deep philosophical art, but a particular instructor may be able to give to his/her classes a philosophical edge that surpasses the stereotypical preaching of the teachers of more "spiritual" arts. Depending on the teacher, classes in an art like Tai Chi may focus on health-maintenance (as most Tai Chi classes do), performance (if trained for looking good in Wushu-styles competitions), self-defense (if the instructor is one of the few stressing combat effectiveness), or competition (if training is primarily in push-hands style competition.)

Although I believe this model can be useful, it is fundamental to remember that models are theoretical tools to help us see reality better. They are not reality itself.

References

Almeida, Bira. *Capoeira: A Brazilian Art Form.* Berkeley: North Atlantic Books, 1986.

Anderson, S. & Jacques B. "The Development of Sambo in Europe and America." *Journal of Asian Martial Arts,* Vol.8 #2, 1999.

Capoeira, Nestor. *The Little Capoeira Book.* Berkeley: North Atlantic Books, 1995.

Cartmell, Tim. *Principles, Analysis, and Application of Effortless Combat Throws.* Pacific Grove: High View Publications, 1996.

Cartmell, Tim. "Internal vs. External: What Sets Them Apart?" *San Soo Journal,* Vol. 4 #1, 1997.

Cartmell, Tim. "From Combat to Sport: Origins and Development of the Martial Arts." *San Soo Journal,* Vol. 3 #2, 1997.

Demura, Fumio. *Bo: Karate Weapons of Self-Defense.* Burbank: Ohara Publications, 1976.

Donohue, John and Kimberley Taylor. "The Classification of the Fighting Arts." *Journal of Asian Martial Arts,* Vol.3 #4, 1994.

Draeger, Donn and Robert W. Smith. *Comprehensive Asian Fighting Arts.* Tokyo: Kodansha International, 1969.

Draeger, Donn. *Classical Budo.* New York: John Weatherhill, Inc., 1973.

Draeger, Donn. *Classical Bujutsu.* New York: John Weatherhill, Inc., 1973.

Draeger, Donn. *Modern Bujutsu and Budo.* New York: John Weatherhill, Inc., 1974.

Henning, Stanley E. "Chinese Boxing: The Internal Versus External Schools in the Light of History & Theory." *Journal of Asian Martial Arts,* Vol. 6 #3, 1997.

Herrigel, Eugen. *Zen in the Art of Archery*. London: Routledge & Kegan Paul Ltd, 1953.

Inosanto, Dan. *The Filipino Martial Arts*. Los Angeles: Know Now, 1980.

Kano, Jigoro. *Kodokan Judo*. New York: Kodansha International, 1986.

Kirby, George. *Jujitsu: Basic Techniques of the Gentle Art*. Santa Clarita (CA): Ohara Publications, 1983.

Liang, Shou-Yu and Tai D. Ngo. *Chinese Fast Wrestling for Fighting: The Art of San Shou Kuai Jiao*. Jamaica Plain: YMAA Publication Center, 1997.

Maliszewski, Michael. *Spiritual Dimensions of the Martial Arts*. Rutland: Charles E. Tuttle Company, 1996.

Miller, Dan. "The Origins of Pa Kua Chang: Part II" *Pa Kua Chang Journal*. High View Publications, Vol. 3 # 2, 1993.

Miller, Dan. "Martial Arts Taught in the Old Tradition (Part I)." *Pa Kua Chang Journal*. High View Publications, Vol. 4 #4, 1994.

Miller, Dan. "Martial Arts Taught in the Old Tradition (Part II): The Deterioration of the Complete Martial Arts System". *Pa Kua Chang Journal*. High View Publications, Vol. 4 #5, 1994.

Poliakoff, Michael B. *Combat Sports in the Ancient World: Competition, Violence, Culture*. New Haven: Yale University Press, 1987.

Reid, Howard and Michael Croucher. *The Way of the Warrior*. London: Eddison/Sadd Editions Limited, 1983.

Stevens, John. *Abundant Peace: The Biography of Morihei Ueshiba, Founder of Aikido*. Boston: Shambala, 1987.

Stevens, John. *The Sword of No-Sword*. Boston: Shambala, 1988.

Sun Lu Tang. *Xing Yi Quan Sue: The Study of Form-Mind Boxing*. Pacific Grove (CA): High View Publications, 1993.

Takagaki, Shinzo and Harold E. Sharp. *The Techniques of Judo*. Rutland (Vermont): Charles E. Tuttle Company, 1998 (1957).

Ueshiba, Kisshomaru. *The Spirit of Aikido*. New York: Kodansha International, 1984.

Ueshiba, Morihei. *Budo: Teachings of the Founder of Aikido*. New York: Kodansha International, 1991.

Weng, Daniel. *Fundamentals of Shuai Chiao: The Ancient Chinese Fighting Art*. Taipei (ROC): Chinese Culture University, 1984.

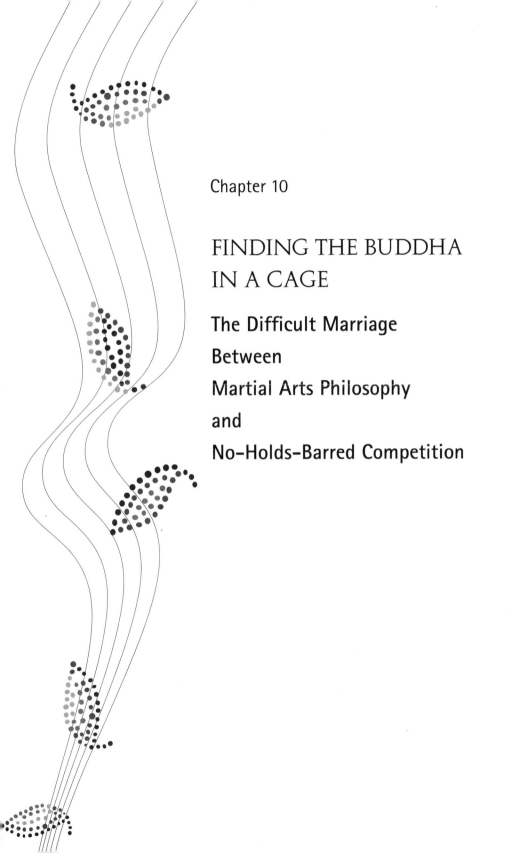

Chapter 10

FINDING THE BUDDHA IN A CAGE

The Difficult Marriage
Between
Martial Arts Philosophy
and
No-Holds-Barred Competition

What we have learned here is that fighting is not what we thought it was.

—Jim Brown (in Shamrock, 1997)

. . . It [the Ultimate Fighting Championship] appeals to the lowest common denominator in our society.

—Arizona Senator John McCain (in Shamrock, 1997)

Only the obtuse are unappreciative of paradox.

—Tom Robbins (in Robbins, 2000)

*F**ew events in modern martial arts history have generated as much uproar as the rise of so-called No-Holds-Barred competitions (I say so-called because after a few rough experiments, all the organizations sponsoring NHB fights rushed to include more restrictive rules, thereby transforming the events in what may be more properly, but less glamorously, termed Many-Holds-Barred competitions.) Hardly any serious martial artist can afford to remain indifferent in the face of something destined to radically change the face of martial arts training. Ever since the debut on pay-per-view of the Ultimate Fighting Championship in 1993, martial artists found themselves divided in two camps: those who labeled NHB competition as a squalid example of blood and gore betraying the true spirit of martial arts, and those who embraced the phenomenon as a much-needed revolution bringing back martial arts to their rightful context. At different times, I have pitched my tent in both camps and came away thinking that— hate it or love it—this is far too interesting a topic for me to pass.*

Peace-loving Buddhist monks in their mountain retreats. Old, wise Asian masters passing secret knowledge to their most deserving disciples. Schools grounded in spirituality as much as in fighting techniques. Combat effectiveness walking hand in hand with the development of a more complete and balanced personality. Warrior-saints who in Ueshiba's style could defeat burly opponents without breaking a sweat while proclaiming that "The Way of the Warrior is to establish harmony." (Ueshiba 1992) This is what used to come to my mind when I thought about martial arts training.

Then, in 1993, I turned on the TV to watch the first much-publicized, no-rules tournament between martial artists from all styles and nations, and my romantic imagination was forced to ask for a time-out. On the screen, monumental masses of muscles, and equally sizable egos, challenged each other in a cage to a competition in which blood-letting and good taste seemed unevenly matched (which one was at an advantage, I leave up to you to decide.) A few seconds into the first fight between Savate champion Gerard Gordeau and Sumo wrestler Teila Tuli, any preconceived idea I had nurtured about martial arts left my mind as soon as Teila Tuli's tooth left his mouth. The rest of the night did not get any better. What had happened to the good old spirituality of martial arts training?

I was puzzled, to say the least. I was in good company, though. If martial artists did not prefer the cheaper counseling offered by a punching bag to the attention of psychotherapists, the screening of the first NHB tournament would have sent thousands of them to visit their favorite shrinks. The event I had witnessed was the beginning of a martial arts revolution. After its passage, no belief would be left unquestioned, no time-honored tradition would go unchallenged, no sacred image would be left in place. All popular stereotypes about the nature of martial arts were about to change. No-Holds-Barred competitions would eventually force many schools—at least those brave enough or stupid enough not to hide their heads in the sand—to seriously review their training methodologies and their ideas about combat effectiveness. Newspapers would compare NHB fights to gladiatorial shows (in case you are wondering, they did not mean it as a compliment.) CNN's Larry King dedicated a show to them. Many states passed laws against them—with Canada going as far as arresting some fighters. A republican senator went on to campaign for their prohibition. NHB fights were big news. Because of them, martial arts broke out of their niche to flirt with the short-attention span of the general population, and thousands of martial artists had to reevaluate everything they thought they knew about the activity to which they dedicated so much of their time and sweat.

But let's go on with order. Before diving into the philosophical questions that NHB fights raised about the nature of martial arts, a brief digression about the history of the phenomenon is needed to better understand what exactly we are talking about.

Video games and movies had been toying with the idea long before reality decided to follow suit. What would happen in a tournament open to all styles of martial arts and, save for a prohibition against eye-gouging and fish-hooking, restricted by almost no rules? All arts claim to be the best one, so what would be the result when only one could walk out backing that claim? Who would come out on top? The idea of a testing ground to prove the worth of different fighting styles had been in the air ever since martial arts had become popular in the West but had never been done in recent history.

Not that this kind of competition lacked illustrious ancestors. At the time of the first Olympic Games in ancient Greece, Pankration, a combat sport combining grappling and striking skills in a format with very few restrictions, was the most important event of all (Poliakoff 1987.) In China, Lei Tai tournaments, in which the martial artists would challenge each other to no-rules fights on elevated platforms, were still around shortly before the advent of the Communist regime.

However, in the twentieth century Western world, no one had yet dared to call the martial artists' bluff and invited them to put their bones and reputations on the line in a tournament open to all styles. It was just a matter of time, though.

The time was November of 1993. Among the men responsible for the event were members of the Gracie clan, a family of Brazilian fighters who had learned Jujitsu from a Japanese immigrant in the early part of the century and had partially modified the style after testing it in hundreds of street-fights and martial arts competitions. In Brazil, the Gracies were fighting legends, but after moving to United States, they quickly found out that their reputation had not made it through customs. In the American imagination, the words "Asian" and "martial arts" were never far away from each other. The best martial artists were mysterious Asian masters whose secret knowledge was no match for anyone else. Even in the tiniest Midwestern town, the local rednecks had heard of Asian martial arts. But a Brazilian martial art?!? Brazil was the land of samba and g-strings. The land of soccer and of the quickly disappearing Amazon jungle. The land of the Carnival and of beaches populated by shapely women of all colors with little patience for clothing. In many people's minds, this was what Brazil was all about. Many good things came from Brazil, but only the most cultured American martial artists knew about Capoeira, the Brazilian art form combining dance and fighting. A Brazilian martial arts master was something that very few in North America were ready to take seriously.

If this was not enough, the Gracies faced another obstacle trying to sell their art in the United States. Americans had learned from movies that—besides being Asian—martial arts were spectacular and flashy. Martial artists were pictured defeating their opponents with flying kicks and acrobatic moves. Since the Gracies offered none of this—their style being primarily focused on the less than spectacular art of groundfighting—they did not fit any of the expectations. Frustrated by several attempts at making a name for themselves in the martial arts community, the Gracies resorted to the method that had built their fame in Brazil: challenge fights against all kinds of martial artists to prove their superiority.

However, this time rather than downsizing the egos of cocky martial artists in their backyard and then letting the voice of the streets build their fame, the Gracies went straight for pay-per-view television. What better way to promote a martial art—an art that, being neither Asian nor spectacular, went against everything people knew martial arts to be—than to win a tournament open to all martial artists and broadcasted to thousands of paying viewers?

The Gracies' desire to prove themselves was the first ingredient in the recipe. Add to this a fortuitous meeting with a fight-promoter. Throw in the mix the very green cash and marketing expertise of a TV producer. Finally, sprinkle the whole thing with the creative genius of John Milius (the man who had written *Apocalypse Now* and directed *Conan The Barbarian*), and the biggest event in modern martial arts history was ready to roll.

Just as 1993 was ready to retire from the calendar, the first Ultimate Fighting Championship took place. Eight fighters from different disciplines faced each other in a direct-elimination tournament inside of an octagonal cage. Following his clan's expectations and against all popular expectations, Royce Gracie, the smallest man to walk in the ring, made short work of the competition and shocked the martial arts world. Just to show that fortune had preciously little to do with his success, Gracie went on to win two of the following three editions of the Ultimate Fighting Championship. With their reputation—and cash register—now restored to their former status, the Gracies took a bow and retired from the UFC before the competition could begin to adjust to their style. Even without its first king, however, the UFC would go on. It had kidnapped the popular imagination and started something that could not be easily stopped.

Over the next few years, the UFC gave rise to a full-blown martial arts revolution. At first, the success of the Gracie's style of groundfighting forced many martial artists to review their ideas about effectiveness in combat. As it became painfully obvious with each new match, those fighters who could only punch and kick but did not know how to play on the ground were regularly taken down and disposed of quickly. This realization sent many martial artists back to the drawing board in order to make up for the deficiencies of their styles of choice. Very soon groundfighting skills alone were not enough either. Strikers learned how to grapple, so grapplers had to learn how to strike. The result was a tribute to Bruce Lee's theory stating that all fighting styles had weaknesses and that only cross-training could produce complete fighters. In this way, in many schools the face of martial arts training changed, and the differences among fighting styles began to fade.

As its promoters quickly figured out, not all the attention that the UFC received was positive. Thousands of people, both martial artists and non-martial artists alike, were disgusted by the seemingly crude aesthetic of UFC fights. Used to the flowery choreography of martial arts movies in which the martial hero could effortlessly defeat several attackers by performing techniques that were both flawless and spectacular, they were shocked to find out how rough real fights were. Especially to the untrained eye, there seemed to be nothing aesthetically beautiful about these fights.

This, however, was not the biggest problem that the UFC had on its hands. Thundering against the moral evil of consenting adults fighting for money, holy crusaders sprung up in many corners to denounce the UFC (and other organizations such as Extreme Fighting which rushed to duplicate UFC-style tournaments) as evidence of the coming end of Western civilization. Many states passed laws to ban NHB tournaments. A republican senator from Arizona, John McCain, went on record to say; "... some of this is so brutal that it is just nauseating.... It appeals to the lowest common denominator in our society. This is something I think there is no place for." (Shamrock 1997)

To be perfectly honest, it is true that UFC fights were fairly violent. How violent? Let's just say that had the UFC teamed up with the American Red Cross, no one in the United States would have been left without blood for transfusions. However, all fighters walked away on their legs, nobody was even remotely close to losing his life, and not a single crippling injury was ever recorded. The same, unfortunately, cannot be said about McCain's favorite sport of Boxing. Of course, like many of his colleagues, McCain was on a first-name basis with hypocrisy and had no problems condemning NHB fights while supporting a sport like Boxing that has directly or indirectly contributed to the deaths of hundreds of fighters in the last few decades. Part of the uproar against the UFC, in fact, came from people close to the boxing industry who were afraid of losing money to a more exciting competitor. Morality was just a good banner for rallying popular support.

Despite its "there-are-no-rules" tough image, NHB fights turned out to be much safer than Boxing. It is not a coincidence that in the ancient Greek Olympics, Wrestling was considered the safest of combat sports, Pankration took second place, whereas Boxing won the prize for the most dangerous of all (Poliakoff 1987.) Although it eludes McCain's notoriously low IQ, the reason for this is simple. By wearing gloves, boxers reduce the likelihood of being forced to stop a fight because of a cut, but in the long run end up taking a more invisible kind of abuse to the brain.

Even more importantly, human nature is not as stupid as I sometimes think. (As a partial excuse for my mistake I offer the fact that before writing this chapter I had to listen to clips of McCain speaking.) No one but a masochist likes to stay toe to toe with an opponent trading punches. After the initial striking flurry, people tend to clinch, often end up on the ground, and, if they have the skills, try to go for chokes and leverages. Within the context of a combat sport, once a submission is applied, the person losing can tap to acknowledge defeat and walk away with a loss but in one piece. In boxing, on the other hand, as soon as the fighters clinch, they are forced to step back and begin striking each other again.

In any case, in time, the UFC eventually agreed to implement increasingly more rules in order to fend off criticisms and legal injunctions, and gain more acceptance as a legitimate sport. (Being accused of being the ruin of Western civilization can do that to you.) For this reason, now UFC fights are divided into rounds and weight classes, prohibit more techniques than they allow, and require competitors to wear some kind of gloves.

Popular opinion, republican senators, and drunken journalists, however, were not the only ones who had been puzzled by the UFC. Thousands of martial artists had been thunderstruck by the event and were trying to understand what to make of it. Some loved it from the start. Others either did not care about it or viewed it as an insult to the spirit of martial arts. Others were stuck somewhere in between; like good Christian girls tormented by the tension between obeying the Ten Commandments and giving in to the sweet feeling tingling up and down their spines as their boyfriends' tongues go on a geographic exploration of the lands surrounding their crucifix-wearing necks. Many martial artists believed the UFC to be the ruin of martial morality yet secretly watched it whenever they could. Forgive me Father for I have sinned, but I have to confess that I counted myself among them.

Besides being motivated by the indoctrination of martial arts instructors who had everything to lose by the popularity of the UFC (since what they taught would have never worked in that context), our moral indignation had strong philosophical roots. The UFC was a showcase for the lowest, most primitive aspects of martial arts. It was a bloody battle that didn't even pretend to justify itself with the sacred principles of martial arts philosophy that we had been taught. It was about fighting for money, winning at all costs, and building monumental egos. It had nothing to do with the forging of a better personality nor with the spirituality of martial arts. It was the ultimate testosterone-driven macho trip. Enter the octagon and use martial arts to prove you are the "baddest" guy there is.

Our response to this was one of disgust. Clap, clap, clap, clap. Now you know how to beat people in a cage. Something to be truly proud of. Does it make you a better person? Does it give you better health? Does it help you in daily life? Is that why you train so many hours a week? To be a sweaty, tough bone-breaking sociopath who can intimidate any prospective opponent? Is this all? If that's it, this is very sad. Any fool with a gun standing ten feet away can blow all your toughness away.

The only reasons why I didn't join the chorus accusing the UFC of ruining Western civilization were that I believed there wasn't much to ruin in that department, and, even if there was, I deeply believed in the right for people to do whatever they wanted with their lives. If fighting in a cage makes you happy, go for it.

Despite this less than promising beginning, my views eventually changed. I'm afraid that with what I'm about to write I'll soon be losing my most soft-hearted, sweeter, philosophically-minded readers. (I'm also afraid that I have already lost my republican readers with my earlier comments about McCain.) But at the risk of finishing this chapter alone, I will confess all of the ugly truth.

No, I have not turned into a bloodthirsty barbarian whose interest in martial arts is focused on learning how to break my neighbors' bones. (The fact that at this very moment my neighbor is blasting the worst kind of *Mariachi* music ever exported north of Tijuana is not helping though.) And yes, I still believe that the philosophical components of martial arts are by far the most interesting and fulfilling parts. However, I can't pretend to forget that, after all is said and done, martial arts are about fighting. All the psychological and philosophical benefits that can be reached thanks to martial arts training are ultimately by-products (beautiful and profound beyond words, but still by-products) of preparing for combat. The desire to free oneself from the very human fear of facing an opponent determined to take our heads off is the primal source of martial arts' philosophical and mental training. Facing this fear and finding ways to overcome it are what brought together a spiritual dimension with what after all was just a method for beating people up.

Despite claims to the contrary, this is how the so-called "spiritual" dimension of martial arts originated. It did not come from peace-loving, "spiritual" guys having new age thoughts in their living rooms. It did not come from wandering monks searching for Nirvana's long-lost address. This is a far too lofty idea of spirituality as well as of human history. Although the day that I'll fail to appreciate the beauty of contradictions is the day when I will volunteer to have a gnome wearing iron shoes dance on my tongue, I can't quite picture these kinds of people wanting to get involved in a sweaty, brutal fighting art in the first place. Spending precious time and energy to learn how to crush another man's limbs is hardly the prerequisite a good pacifist needs on his/her resume.

No, the spiritual dimension of martial arts originated with a very different kind of crowd. It came from fighters who were terrified of death at the hands of the enemy. Knowing that fear does nothing but paralyze and make one weaker, these martial artists had to find a way to discipline their minds and conquer their fears in order to give themselves an extra chance to survive on the battlefield (Westenbrook 1999.) Zen meditation, for example, was the tool used by many Japanese samurai to prevent their fear of death from rendering them powerless during a fight (Suzuki 1959, Maliszewski 1996.) The accidental result was that some of those warriors had the wisdom to realize that the mental training was not helpful simply as a means to avoid getting killed in battle (which in and of itself was a good start,) but also—by pressing the "mute" button on the voice of one's fears—enriched their daily lives. All the beautiful philosophical stuff that today makes the existence of thousands of martial artists more enjoyable is a side effect of facing one's fear of combat.

Furthermore, if we keep in mind that UFC-style competitions are not the ultimate goal of martial arts training, but simply one possible part, what's wrong with them? As it is, most martial artists tend to talk too much about how their art would work if they had to really use it. Lacking a concrete test, everyone can make outlandish claims without fear of having to concretely back up their words with actions. Without a testing ground, it is easy to slip into fantasy-land and lose track of what really does and does not work. This is why the martial arts world is full of charlatans who can talk much more than they can act. Among the reasons why the UFC offended many martial artists is the fact that it forced them to prove their theories through a concrete test. With a wonderfully empirical approach, the UFC said, "Let's keep the game honest. Enough with the talk. Let's see what you can really do."

Of course, a sport, even the most extreme sport like the UFC-style fighting, is not the real thing. Fighting one-on-one in a ring is not the same thing as fighting in the street. However, if effectiveness is one of the goals of your martial arts practice (not that is has to be since martial arts offer so much else, but if it is), UFC-style competitions (or more delicate forms of sparring) are perfect labs where to test one's skills while facing one's fears.

Having said this, of course I am not claiming that competitions like the UFC—by pitting martial artists against their fears in the most extreme possible setting but still within the limits of reasonable safety—are profound spiritual events. Call me prejudiced, call me superficial, but a man like UFC veteran Tank Abbott, a beer-guz-zling, street-fighting, proudly self-proclaimed member of the numerous but less than reputable category collectively known as white trash, doesn't strike me as the most spiritual guy I can think of. I am also not claiming that, in order to access martial arts' deepest aspects, everyone should put their physical wellbeing on the line and enter the cage for a NHB fight. However, I have moved away from my initial self-righteous indignation against UFC style fighting and don't believe anymore that these competitions are a betrayal of the true spirit of martial arts. The Buddha's favorite hang-out spot may not be the cage, but I wouldn't rule out the possibility of finding him there. After all, the good man was much less discriminating than most "spiritual" people like to think.

References:

Homer. *The Iliad of Homer* (translated by Richard Lattimore). Chicago: University of Chicago Press, 1961 [1951].

Lee, Bruce. "Liberate Yourself from Classical Karate" in *Black Belt* magazine. Burbank: Ohara, 1971.

Lee, Bruce. *The Tao of Jeet Kune Do.* Burbank: Ohara, 1975.

Maliszewski, Michael. *Spiritual Dimension of the Martial Arts.* Ruthland: Charles E. Tuttle, 1996.

Poliakoff, Michael B. *Combat Sports in the Ancient World: Competition, Violence, Culture.* New Haven: Yale University Press, 1987.

Robbins, Tom. *Fierce Invalids Home from Hot Climates.* New York: Bantam Books, 2000.

Shamrock, Ken and Richard Hanner. *Inside the Lion's Den: The Life and Submission Fighting System of Ken Shamrock.* Boston: Charles E. Tuttle Co., Inc, 1997.

Suzuki, Daisetz Teitaro. *Zen and Japanese Culture.* New York: Pantheon Books, 1959.

Ueshiba, Morihei. *The Art of Peace: Teachings of the Founder of Aikido* (ed. John Stevens). Boston: Shambala, 1992.

Westbrook, Adele and Oscar Ratti. *Secrets of the Samurai: A Survey of the Martial Arts of Feudal Japan.* Edison (NJ): Castle Books 1999 [1973].

Chapter 11

EPISTEMOLOGICAL ANARCHISM

The Philosophy of Jeet Kune Do

... whoever heeds commands does not heed himself. Break, break, you lovers of knowledge, the old tablets!
—Friedrich Nietzsche (Nietzsche 1995)

[I am] a man who wishes nothing more than daily to lose some reassuring belief, who seeks and finds his happiness in this daily greater liberation of the mind.
—Friedrich Nietzsche (Nietzsche 1995)

I must invent my own systems or else be enslaved by other men's.
—William Blake quoted in *Another Roadside Attraction* by Tom Robbins (Robbins 1971)

INTRODUCTION

Almost thirty years after his death in 1973, no martial artist has gotten even close to achieving half of his popularity. Far from fading from memory, his legacy still inspires the enthusiasm of the masses. Frozen in time by a premature death, his image has been printed over and over again on the covers of magazines throughout the world. Long past are the days when his work almost single-handedly changed the way in which Asian Americans were viewed in the United States, gave Chinese people a tremendous boost of self-esteem, and opened the road to Hollywood for other Asian actors. Gone the days when his movies made the fortune of scalpers who could sell a $2 ticket for $45 or when, in some countries, his titles had to be withdrawn from theatres to ease traffic jams (Little 1996). However, judging from his enduring fame, the passing of a few decades has only contributed to turn the man into something bigger than life. Even today, he is the patron saint of martial arts magazines. In lean times, when the financial future seems bleak, a martial arts magazine only needs to dedicate the cover article to him in order to bounce back and bring up the sales. In the popular imagination, he was not just another martial artist. He was The Martial Artist. For countless people around the globe, his name has become the symbol for martial arts as a whole.

The man, of course, is Bruce Lee. In case I needed further proof, a recent experience reminded me of just how far-reaching Lee's fame is. In this instance, a department chair from California State University at Hayward recommended me to consider teaching a course entitled "Bruce Lee: An American Icon." By itself this proposal, coming from a serious scholar of a respected academic institution who bears no personal interest in the martial arts, speaks volumes. What Lee was able to do, in fact, was to fascinate many different kinds of people for very different motives.

For the same reason why Western movies have attracted millions of viewers, Lee's role as a tough, lonely hero who fights injustice wherever he meets it is certainly appealing to vast segments of the public. Lee, however, added to this role an aesthetic beauty and a philosophical depth which were lacking in most of the Old West's gunfighters. In this way, he managed to intrigue even those people (including considerable numbers of women) who are turned off by excessive displays of guns, testosterone and machismo. It is undeniable that Lee's acting career was centered on beating people up, but he had something going for him that was different from everyone else. He had style. When other people fought, viewers would only see a fight. When Lee fought, it was poetry in motion. Martial, but also art.

Lee's popularity, however, has done nothing to endear him to the serious scholars of the martial arts who view him as little more than the inspiration for thousands of obnoxiously bad martial arts movies. In this sense, the absence of any article about Bruce Lee in the Journal of Asian Martial Arts, which is one of the only, if not the only, forum for high-quality scholarship on the martial arts, is very telling. After all, when any fool who knows nothing about martial arts can quote every line from Bruce Lee's movies, it is understandable that experts may decide to dismiss Lee's work as a shallow example of pop-culture.

In my opinion, however, that would be a big, big mistake. Unlike all other actors with iron-hard abs and flashy kicks who, once their fifteen minutes of fame are up, are not worth a minute of our time,

Lee has something else to offer. Although I certainly do not believe that popularity is a good measure of depth, the fact that Lee is adored by legions of fans from several different generations, many of whom could not care less about the martial arts, may suggest that his appeal relies on something deeper than a popular infatuation with Asian fighting styles.

A clue to what exactly this "something" may be lies at the foot of Lee's tombstone. There, engraved in stone, is a single sentence left by his friends and disciples, "Your Inspiration Continues To Guide Us Toward Our Personal Liberation." This hardly sounds like a statement that is likely to be placed at the foot of Van Damme's tombstone (my apologies to Van Damme for picking on him) or at the foot of just about any other actor/martial artist's tombstone. If Bruce Lee were just another athlete or another Hollywood celebrity, I honestly doubt that he could inspire or guide anyone towards much of anything, let alone personal liberation. What inspired those who came in contact with him was something entirely different than the glamour of movie stardom. The answer to what this thing may be can be found in a revealing passage by Lee's widow, Linda Lee Cadwell, "What is this *something* about Bruce Lee that continues to fascinate people in all walks of life? I believe it is the depth of his personal philosophy, which subconsciously, or otherwise, projects from the screen and through his writings." (Little 1996)

The same feeling is echoed in the comments of Lee's own students. Basketball superstar Kareem Abdul Jabbar, who studied martial arts under Lee's guidance and appeared in one of his movies, declared, "He was a teacher first of all. He taught philosophy and tried to spread knowledge and wisdom. That's why he took on the martial arts establishment the way he did." (Ibidem) And Tai Chi master, Daniel Lee, also a student of Bruce Lee, similarly stated, "This [Lee's] was a different approach to martial arts instruction. We studied philosophy with Bruce because he had philosophy as his underlying theme and direction. He was really my mentor in showing the linkage between philosophy and martial art. They're inseparable." (Ibidem) Besides these comments made by people who knew him well, Lee's personal library, made up of over 2,500 books, mostly about philosophy and martial arts, is another good indicator of his commitment to philosophical inquiry.

In case these pieces of evidence are not convincing enough, and the idea of Bruce Lee as a philosopher still seems too far-fetched, we only need to examine the concepts at the root of Jeet Kune Do, the martial art created by Lee, to see how fundamental philosophy was to Lee's approach to the martial arts. Rather than setting itself up to be a new martial arts style with its codified set of unique forms and techniques, Jeet Kune Do advocates the elimination of styles in favor of a constant process of individual research aimed at finding the techniques and training methods that best fit one's needs. Anytime the practitioner of JKD finds something effective along the way, or decides that a certain technique does not work for him/her, he or she is free to change the art.

Seen in this perspective, clearly, more than a new martial art in the traditional sense of the word, Jeet Kune Do appears to be a philosophical principle applied to the martial arts. The creation of a martial art based on such antiauthoritarian, nearly anarchist thinking points out that Lee may have more in common with philosophers like Feyerabend, Lao Tzu, and Krishnamurti than with entertainers like Jackie Chan, Sammo Hung, or Jean Claude Van Damme.

NOT NEW, YET NEW

Although this chapter has so far been introducing the idea that Lee's philosophy may have been his greatest contribution, if we want to be perfectly honest we also have to acknowledge something that Bruce Lee's aficionados usually do not like to admit. As a philosopher, Lee did not come up with any original ideas. The entire philosophy so passionately espoused by Lee derives from the writings of other people. Had someone explained the concepts of royalties and copyright to Lao Tzu and Chuang Tzu, the semi-mythological authors of the most famous Taoist writings, their descendants would now be swimming in gold while lifting their best champagne glasses to Lee's memory. In fact, the vast majority of the ideas widely popularized by Lee are taken directly from Taoist sources. Even the emblem chosen by Lee for his art of Jeet Kune Do is a slightly modified version of the Taoist Yin/Yang symbol.

Besides Taoism, Lee's most obvious sources include Zen Buddhism (which is itself partially inspired by Taoist ideas), and the writings of modern philosophers such as Krishnamurti and Alan Watts. Even if we limit ourselves only to the field of martial arts, Lee's approach is not entirely new. For example, his idea of freeing ourselves from the unnatural constraints of codified styles was expressed decades before Lee's time by one of the greatest Chinese martial artists of the early part of the twentieth century, the creator of I-Chuan, Wang Hsiang Chai (Cartmell 1998).

By stating that on a philosophical level Lee did not really create anything, am I trying to contradict my own initial position and, in a gesture of Socratic perversion, now arguing for its opposite? Not at all. Paradoxes are the essence of Taoism, and since Taoism is what we are dealing with here, we should not be surprised to stumble upon what seems to be a contradiction.

Suggesting that someone made great philosophical contributions even though he clearly did not commit to paper a single original philosophical idea is not as absurd as it may sound. For example, Alan Watts, who is considered by some as one of the most important philosophers of the twentieth century and who greatly inspired Lee, did not invent anything new either. His books (which I strongly recommend to anyone who has not yet had the pleasure of reading them) are based almost entirely on Taoist and Buddhist ideas. However, despite being clearly derivative, his writings beautifully convey the essence of Taoism and Buddhism in a completely new, original way. Although the topic and the conclusions found in Watt's books are not new, the freshness of his style, analogies, anecdotes and examples infuse new life to them. Furthermore, the way in which Watts adapted Taoist and Buddhist philosophies to a Western mentality is a splendid illustration of philosophical creativity.

In a similar fashion, Bruce Lee took old ideas and applied them in new, original ways. He took Taoism and Buddhism and applied them to the competitive, ego-driven world of movie-making, to the martial arts and to his own daily life. In the process, he drastically altered the Western perception of Asian cultures, and inspired many martial artists to explore the philosophical dimension at the root of their physical practice. In the 1960s and early 1970s, Lee's philosophical stance, popularized through his writings and his movies, was an antiauthoritarian slap in the face to the dogma and immutable tradition that still dominated the way most people practiced martial arts in the West. Although, as we have seen earlier, he was not the first to challenge the dogmatism of some martial arts schools, he was more visible and more radical than anyone who had come before him, and therefore was also in a more powerful position to affect the prevailing perceptions of martial arts' practice and philosophy.

Having so far made the case that Lee's philosophy deserves our attention, the reminder of this chapter will explore the ideological context from which Jeet Kune Do emerged and the theoretical principles on which the art is based.

THE BREAK WITH CHINESE TRADITION

Since earlier I remarked that Lee derived his entire philosophy from Taoist and Buddhist sources, readers may get the mistaken impression that Lee's approach was consistent with Chinese traditions. Nothing could be further from the truth. Without a doubt, Taoism and Buddhism have greatly affected Chinese culture. Chinese medicine, for example, is fully rooted in Taoist ideas (Maciocia 1989). Supposedly, Bodhidharma, the mythological father of Shaolin kung fu, was an Indian monk also credited with introducing Ch'an Buddhism to China. Before Communism made finding a fully functioning religious temple as unlikely as running into a giant panda dancing in the streets of Beijing, Taoist and Buddhist monasteries filled the country. However, the forms of Taoism and

Buddhism that enjoyed such vast popular following for great part of Chinese history were not the same kind of Taoism and Buddhism which inspired Lee.

Most scholars of Asian religions distinguish between the early philosophical Taoism presented in classics such as the *Tao Te Ching* and *the Chuang Tzu* and the later forms of popular Taoism which provided the basis for much of Chinese folk religion (Smith 1991, Wright 1959). Elusive poetry, beautiful paradoxes and a nearly complete lack of concern with gods characterized the philosophical Taoism which provided the basis for Lee's philosophy. Rituals, prayers to the Gods, an alchemical quest for immortality, and the attempt to enlist spirits to one's help characterized the popular forms of religious Taoism practiced by most Chinese people.

In a similar way, Buddha's own teachings, which were favored by Lee, were much more uncompromising than the teachings passed on by most forms of Chinese popular Buddhism. For example, Buddha invited people to find out the truth for themselves rather than follow any religious authority, and to work for their own salvation without relying on gods, prayers or rituals (Smith 1991). Chinese popular Buddhism, on the other hand, heavily emphasized prayers, rituals, devotion to Buddha and to the bodhisatvas, and obedience to the top of the religious hierarchy (Wright 1959).

As we can see, then, Lee's love for philosophical Taoism and for the most radical aspects of Buddha's teachings was hardly in line with the diluted and simplified forms of Taoism and Buddhism favored by the masses. His philosophical outlook was therefore more at odds with Chinese tradition than consistent with it.

Furthermore, another element contributes to distance Lee's approach from Chinese tradition. Chinese thought, in fact, has been heavily influenced by another philosophical current which is even more antithetical to Lee's worldview than popular forms of Taoism and Buddhism: Confucianism. Whereas the philosophical Taoism and the Buddhism embraced by Lee can be subtle and paradoxical, Confucianism offers the security of precise formulas and simple, straightforward rules. Philosophical Taoism requires great sensitivity to be grasped. Confucianism is very easy to follow. Philosophical Taoism mocks rigid laws. Confucianism reveres them. Confucian ideology dictates the rules of proper behavior, establishes the reciprocal, but unequal obligations between family members, regulates the relationship between citizens and state authorities, and oversees every possible aspect of public life. In other words, the very matrix of Chinese society was and still is saturated with Confucianism.

With its emphasis on intellectual virtues and its disdain for anything physical as unworthy of a scholar, Confucianism has been primarily responsible for the low esteem in which until a few decades ago martial arts were held among the more educated, upper classes, and for the ambivalence that Chinese society as a whole felt toward martial artists (Miller 1993). Also, with its reverence for the old, traditional ways and its high praise of filial piety, obedience to the elders, and ancestor worship, Confucianism has filled Chinese thought with deeply conservative tendencies.

In Lee's philosophy, not a trace of Confucianism can be found. Rather, as we will see more in detail later, Lee stood in firm opposition to the most dogmatic aspects of Chinese tradition cherished by Confucianism. By rejecting Confucianism and choosing to embrace the antiauthoritarian viewpoint of philosophical Taoism, Lee allied himself with the fringe-dwellers, the outcasts, the mavericks, the philosophical outlaws, the misfits of Chinese culture. In fact, although some of the principles of philosophical Taoism have been incorporated into Chinese culture, its radical nature makes it appealing to only a minority of people and sets it apart from the traditions on which most of Chinese society is based.

One clear example of Lee's rebellion against Confucian ideals can be found before we even look into the actual contents of his philosophical writings. According to Confucian standards, in fact, Lee committed an unforgivable sin. He took credit for creating the art of Jeet Kune Do. Even if Jeet Kune Do principles were not as uncompromisingly opposed to Confucianism as they are, the very act of claiming authorship of a new approach to the martial arts was unacceptable by Confucian standards.

Since Western society highly praises individual initiative and innovation, Western readers may wonder how taking credit for one's creation can be considered negatively. In Chinese martial arts, however, innovation is rarely looked upon kindly. Creating something new inevitably implies that one is at least partially departing from tradition. And tradition is exactly what Confucianism exalts. The way of the ancestors—according to Confucianism—is the best possible one. Therefore any departure from the traditions passed down since ancient times cannot but make things worse. Viewed through Confucian lenses, creating means losing the perfection of the ancient ways.

For this reason, it had been customary for Chinese martial artists wishing to create a new art to mask it in a more traditional and acceptable garb. Rather than claiming authorship, the right thing to do in order to have one's creation accepted was to attribute the new style to an old, respected source. By connecting the art to a famous lineage, the chances of receiving a good reception were substantially increased. Much in the same way in which ancient Greek poets often attributed their creations to Homer, the most famous and beloved of Greek poets, (thereby choosing personal anonymity but raising the possibility that their creation would gain fame), Chinese martial artists often pretended to have learned the new style from a mysterious descendant of one of the mythological heroes of the pantheon of Chinese martial arts.

For example, when in the 1600s Chi Long Feng began teaching Xing-i, he said that he had learned the style from a manuscript authored by Yue Fei, the twelfth century legendary general who had defeated the armies of China's northern enemies (www.shenwu.com). In the same way, when in the late nineteenth century Tung Hai Chuan created the art of Pa Kua Chang, he declared that he had learned the style from a secret sect of anonymous mountain-dwelling Taoists (a good substitute for a famous name) (Miller 1993). Later on, when Kao I-Sheng changed the Pa Kua curriculum by incorporating elements from other arts, he similarly told the story that he had learned this new version of the art from some mysterious Taoist hermit. (If one is to believe these stories, the abundance of mysterious Taoist hermits in the history of martial arts seems to suggest that they made up the majority of the Chinese population). (Miller 1994). Even the fact that, despite a nearly complete lack of concrete evidence, Tai Chi Chuan is popularly attributed to the Taoist Chang San Feng and Shaolin Kung Fu to Bodhidharma is probably caused by the desire to attribute the creation of a new style to a character of mythological stature.

After examining all these examples, we may now appreciate the significance of Lee's refusal to present his creation in a traditional fashion. Had Lee disappeared for a few years and had later told that he had been the disciple of an old Taoist, he would have conformed to a culturally approved way of introducing innovations. By claiming credit, on the other hand, he rejected the importance of lineage, did not even pretend to follow tradition, and therefore challenged a time-honored custom. At the time when Lee introduced Jeet Kune Do, he was a twenty-eight years old actor who lived in United States, only had a few years of formal training under a recognized master (Wing Chun's Yip Man), and had never received a teaching license. Yet, he claimed that following the old ways was useless and that his own approach made more sense. Not exactly the kind of comments designed to keep down the blood pressure of Confucius' followers.

IF YOU MEET THE BUDDHA, KILL HIM: JKD'S ALLERGY FOR AUTHORITY

If we move from the way in which Lee presented Jeet Kune Do to the actual contents of the art, the chances of raising Confucian enthusiasms decrease even further. Lee's philosophy, in fact, amounts to a declaration of war against the conservative, dogmatic tendencies encouraged by Confucianism. An example representative of Lee's approach can be found in the following passage from an article written by Lee for *Black Belt* magazine.

> Unfortunately, most students in the martial arts are conformists. Instead of learning to depend on themselves for expression, they blindly follow their instructors, no longer feeling alone, and finding security in mass imitation. The product of this imitation is a dependent mind. Independent inquiry, which is essential to genuine understanding, is sacrificed. Look around the martial arts and witness the assortment of routine performers, trick artists, desensitized robots, glorifiers of the past, and so on-all followers or exponents of organized despair." (Lee 1971)

As we can clearly see from this passage, according to Lee one does not learn by simply following a formula laid out by someone else. Rather than revering the way of the ancestors and accepting their conclusions as absolute truths, Lee encouraged individuals to question everything and find out for themselves. Whereas Confucianism valued obedience and conformity, Lee emphasized creativity and freedom. As Lee himself wrote, "Art lives where absolute freedom is, because where it is not, there can be no creativity." (Lee 1975) Lee's commitment to individual freedom and empowerment placed him in opposition to any tradition requiring uncritical loyalty to authority.

In his quest for self-liberation, Lee had many models to draw from. Philosophical Taoism was certainly one of them. "The more taboos and inhibitions there are in the world, the poorer the people become" (Lao Tzu 1989) is one of the many Taoist battle cries against authority that Lee paraphrased several times in his books and articles.

Indian philosopher Jiddu Krishamurti was another of Lee's sources of inspiration. Acclaimed as a messiah since birth, Krishamurti grew up adored and revered by members of a religious organization who believed that he was the ultimate savior they had been waiting for. Once he grew up, however, Krishnamurti kissed good-by to their messianic dreams, declining his role and inviting people to become their own saviors. Because of his actions and anti-authoritarian worldview, Krishnamurti was included by Lee among his main philosophical influences (Lee 1975).

Buddha was also one of Lee's role models. Born as the son of a king at the peak of the Hindu social scale, Buddha renounced it all to give his heart and soul to the ascetic practices of Hinduism. When these practices failed to bring the desired results, Buddha did not hesitate to abandon Hindu traditions and walk off the beaten path. His successful attempt to reach enlightenment outside the confines of tradition convinced him that blind allegiance to the old ways was an obstacle on the path to liberation. From then on, Buddha spread the subversive fire of a religion devoid of rigid authority. Suggesting that the gods had better things to do than playing with humans and that the Brahmins and their old rituals could not help people achieve nirvana, Buddha went against some of the most basic beliefs of Hindu society. As if this rebellion against the status quo were not enough, Buddha also went against another social convention by accepting to teach women and people of the lower classes.

Even more revolutionary, however, was the fact that Buddha did not ask people to believe him, but encouraged them to find the truth for themselves. In his view, belief could not liberate anyone. Only direct experience could. For this reason, Buddha saw himself more as a guide pointing the way than as a king imposing a law. Buddha's allegedly last words, "Work out your own salvation with diligence," perfectly express his invitation for people to trust themselves more than any external authority (Smith 1991). Most forms of Buddhism created after Buddha's death downplayed the antiauthoritarian aspects of Buddha's message because it was simply too extreme and too frightening for most people to deal with. Taking charge of one's own life and making all the decisions alone is much harder than following an established way. It requires more courage than most people can ever hope to have. For this reason, it became much easier for people to worship Buddha and turn him into another object of veneration than to follow his example and create their own path (Smith 1991).

One of the few religious currents that did not ignore these unsettling aspects of Buddha's message was Zen Buddhism. By warning students against the dangers of dogmatism and inviting them to question authority, Zen statements such as, "If you meet the Buddha, kill him" may paradoxically honor Buddha's example more than any of the prayers to Buddha recited by some other Buddhist schools. Since Zen is one of the few schools of Buddhism that to a great extent emphasizes freedom from blind devotion, it should not come as a surprise that Lee's own writings are flooded with Zen references.

As we will soon see, the antiauthoritarian ideas championed by the sources mentioned above helped Lee shape an approach to the martial arts that went against the way in which most martial arts were practiced and taught in the West. Besides rejecting many of the formalities surrounding martial arts practice such as the elaborate bowing, the belt system, the use of special uniforms, the dojo hierarchy, the almost religious subservience to the instructor, and the many other ritualistic components that characterized some martial arts schools in United States, Lee addressed even more fundamental, methodological questions. One of them was something that most martial artists of the time took for granted and never thought of questioning: the very concept of separate martial arts styles with their separate sets of rules, and separate teaching methodologies.

MARTIAL ARTS STYLES AS IDEOLOGICAL PRISONS: FREEDOM FROM "BELONGING"

Anyone who has ever been involved in the martial arts has probably, at one time or another, participated in the never-ending discussions about the merits or demerits of each martial art style. It is not uncommon for these kind of discussions to quickly degenerate into full-scale arguments in which practitioners of each style defend the virtue of their art of choice while denigrating the validity of all others. Much like religious fundamentalists claim that all spiritual paths other than their own ("the one true faith") are misguided, martial artists often play the "my-style-is-better-than-yours" game and try to assert that they are right while everyone else is wrong.

According to Bruce Lee, the apologists of particular martial arts styles, irrespective of which style they belong to, are all wrong. Lee, in fact, argued that by turning personal intuitions and sound principles into absolute laws equal for everyone, all styles are guilty of turning partial truths into the only Truth and thereby failing to see the complete range of possible truths. The following series of quotations, taken from Lee's own writings, can offer a clear testimony of Lee's very controversial stance about martial art styles.

> Styles tend to … separate people—because they each have their own doctrine, and then the doctrine becomes their gospel of truth that you cannot change. But if you do not have styles, if you just say "Here I am, as a human being— how can I express myself totally and completely?" if you can do this, then you won't create a style, because style is a crystallization. (Lee 1975)

> Once conditioned in a partialized method, once isolated in an enclosing pattern, the practitioner faces his opponent through a screen of resistance—he is "performing" his stylized blocks and listening to his own screaming and not seeing what the opponent is really doing. (Ibidem)

> Classical forms dull your creativity, condition and freeze your sense of freedom. You no longer "be", but merely "do", without sensitivity. (Ibidem)

> When in a split second, your life is threatened, do you say, "Let me make sure my hand is on my hip, and my style is 'the' style"? When your life is in danger, do you argue about the method you will adhere to while saving yourself? Why the duality? (Ibidem)

The second-hand artist blindly following his sensei or sifu accepts his pattern. As a result, his action and, more importantly, his thinking become mechanical. His responses become automatic, according to set patterns, making him narrow and limited. (Lee 1971)

It is conceivable that a long time ago a certain martial artist discovered some partial truth. During his lifetime, the man resisted the temptation to organize this partial truth, although this is a common tendency in man's search for security and certainty in life. After his death, his students took "his" hypothesis, "his" postulates, "his" inclination, and "his" method and turned them into law. Impressive creeds were then invented, solemn reinforcing ceremonies prescribed, rigid philosophy and patterns formulated, and so on, until finally an institution was erected. So what originated as one man's intuition of some sort of personal fluidity was transformed into solidified, fixed knowledge, complete with organized, classified responses presented in a logical order. In so doing, the well-meaning, loyal followers not only made this knowledge a holy shrine but also a tomb in which they buried the founder's wisdom. (Ibidem)

All styles require adjustment, partiality, denials, condemnation, and a lot of self-justification. The solutions they purport to provide are the very cause of the problem because they limit and interfere with our natural growth and obstruct the way to genuine understanding. Divisive by nature, styles keep men apart from each other rather than unite them. (Ibidem)

As we can see, Lee wasted little love on traditional martial arts schools. Before moving on to examine what kind of methodology Lee advocated instead of following established "styles," however, it is worth pausing for a minute to consider the incredibly revolu-

tionary implications of his critique of the very concept of "style."
By questioning the loyalty of martial artists to their own particular
schools of fighting (Karate, Jujitsu, Kung fu, Aikido, Judo, and the
other myriad of styles and sub-styles of martial arts ever devised),
Lee was doing more than suggesting a methodological change. He
was grappling with one of the most powerful forces in human history: people's sense of identity.

It was as if he had questioned people's loyalty to their own country, or to their own religion. One simply does not question such
things. Doing so would be unpatriotic and blasphemous. Normally,
group identity is reinforced through passionate adherence to a
common set of beliefs and through consensus among members.
Questioning the core beliefs on which a group is based (whether the
group is a religious sect, a political organization, a street gang, or
martial arts style makes no difference) is at best a dangerous threat
to the common sense of identity, and at worst, an act of insubor-
dination and betrayal. Lee went even further. He did not simply
criticize the core beliefs of one particular group. Rather, he questioned the very idea of adhering to any particular group. According to Lee, the simple act of joining a group structured around a
codified set of rules and beliefs ends up creating a "we-against-
them" mentality, causing endless divisions and useless conflicts with
those who rally under a different flag.

If we stop to test Lee's hypothesis against the backdrop of
human history, the results are frightening. Racism, mass enslave-
ment of people with a different skin color, witch hunts, inquisi-
tions, political persecutions of ideological dissidents, gang wars,
"holy" wars justified in the name of religious differences, wars rooted
in ethnic pride, wars fought by combatants who do not understand
the causes of the conflict but who fight nonetheless in the name
of their country.... The number of massacres and the amount suffering caused by the human predisposition to fight over perceived
differences can hardly be calculated.

At the origin of all this bloodshed, very often, is the human
need to belong and be part of a group. The promise of a common

dream and a common identity is one of the main reasons for the popularity of churches, street gangs, and of any other kind of exclusive organizations. "Your dreams are our dreams—the voice of the group reassures us—We understand you because we are like you. We will protect you. We will love you as one of us. We are like a big family. You can depend on us. We are always there for you. If you have a doubt, we can comfort you and give you all the answers you need. If you play by our rules, you will never be alone again."

Few are the human beings who do not like to hear these messages. As any good demagogue looking to build a strong following knows, a powerful dream, a flag, and a set of symbols are the perfect magnets around which people can gather to escape the fear of being alone by building a common sense of identity. In fact, facing life's tragedies alone, filled with insecurities and with no one to turn to, is not what most people want. Having someone who chooses for us, provides the answers to all the questions, and makes us feel part of something bigger than ourselves is the perfect cure for those who need guidance (that is to say, just about every human being possessing anything less than tremendous self-confidence).

Since there can be no concept of "we" if there is no "them" representing the antithesis of everything that "we" stand for, group identity inevitably is built on opposition to something. It is not a coincidence that patriotism always runs stronger in times of war. (Not surprisingly, in Lee's mind, patriotism, just like any other value emphasizing the power of the group over the individual, is among the diseases to be eliminated) (Ibidem). The existence of a common enemy is the fuel feeding the fire of a group's own sense of identity. This is perhaps the reason why human history, in every part of the world, is filled with ideologically justified bloodbaths.

By questioning the concept of loyalty to any particular style, Lee took the bull of group identity by the horns and challenged the sensibility of the human desire to belong. Why belong to any school of thought—Lee asked—if all that it does is divide us into opposing factions and prevent us from seeing the truth of different points of view? Our reassuring sense of identity—Lee seemed to suggest—is nothing but a comfortable prison shielding us from the intensity of unfiltered experience. It shields us from many of the dangers and doubts of life as well as from the ecstasy and the beauty of it all. Through preconceptions and dogmas, most organizations shape the quality of our experiences, force us to watch life through the lenses of an ideological form of tunnel vision and ultimately end up limiting the range of our choices. Too afraid to bear the weight of choosing on their own, many people hide behind the security of a group that provides all the answers. According to Lee, however, this is a way to hide, not a way to live.

Lee would probably agree with Tibetan meditation master Chogyam Trungpa when he said "The key to warriorship ... is not being afraid of who you are." (Trungpa 1988) Being fearlessly willing to make mistakes in the process of making one's own choices free from any dogma is the only path that Lee advocated. Much more than a methodological change, Lee's challenge to martial arts styles should therefore be seen as a challenge to do what people are most scared of doing: refusing to submit to the power of any superior authority, and taking full responsibility as the leader of their own lives.

USING NO WAY AS THE WAY: LEE'S EPISTEMOLOGICAL ANARCHISM

In contrast to the approach preached by many schools of martial arts, Lee argued that the art should serve the individual rather than the individual serving the art (Maliszewski 1990). In one of his most famous quotes, Lee declared; "Man, the living, creating individual, is always more important than any established style." (Lee 1971) What this translated to in practical terms was a radical departure from the methodology normally used by martial arts schools. Rather than following the standard curriculum of an established style, Lee began advocating a form of cross-training aimed at picking the best from different martial arts styles. In this way, Lee moved away from the Wing Chun style that he had learned in Hong Kong from Yip Man and established his own "non-style" of Jeet Kune Do.

Most great innovators in the history of the martial arts cross-trained in several arts, and created a new style by taking techniques, exercises and ideas from different sources and molding them into a new system. Lee, however, took matters one step further. Rather than establishing a new style, he created a major controversy by suggesting that martial artists should be constantly involved in a process of research that never crystallizes its findings into a finished product.

Although in the last few years, the popularity of no-holds-barred events such as the Ultimate Fighting Championship has convinced many martial artists of the necessity to cross-train, in the late 1960s, when Lee first spoke out, the idea of cross-training was not so easily received. In order to understand why Lee's approach was so inflammatory, we need to remember that most schools of martial arts of the time (and many schools of martial arts even today) advocated never changing the style they practiced. According to them, since the style had been perfected by great masters in ancient times, changing the art in any way would be an arrogant mistake bound to water-down its effectiveness. Only by training precisely following the guidelines passed on by the masters, could one hope to come close to their unsurpassed skills.

In the same way as Confucianism stressed the importance of imitating the way of the ancestors without ever introducing any change, many martial arts schools considered the idea of changing any part of their training as a betrayal of the traditions upon which their style was founded. Considering that this was the dominant philosophy among many martial artists, we can imagine the effect of Lee's public rejection of traditional styles with statements such as, "The classical man is just a bundle of routine, ideas and tradition. When he acts, he is translating every living moment in terms of the old." (Lee 1975)

Whereas Confucianism and most martial arts schools preached the meticulous conservation of the purity of the old ways, Lee believed that the very attempt to conserve anything killed any purity that may have originally been there. As Taoism clearly pointed out, only by changing and flowing, could water remain pure. When still, a body of water inevitably turns into a swamp. Believing that the same analogy applied to human affairs, Lee thought that any attachment to the past was a hindrance to living in the present. "To understand and live *now*—Lee wrote—everything of yesterday must die." (Ibidem) Just like the Taoist writers, Heraclitus, one of the most famous pre-Socratic Greek philosophers, unequivocally stated that everything is constantly changing (Wheelwright 1959).

Following this line of thought, Lee argued that no fixed formula could capture the flow of existence. What worked yesterday may not work today. What the old masters discovered was one way to fight, not necessarily the only one, or even the best one. Different conditions call for different approaches. To Lee, an endless process of trial and error was therefore preferable to establishing one's day intuition as an immutable law. Instilling in his students the ability to adapt to any situation made much more sense to Lee than teaching them a fixed method of fighting. The following quotations, clearly inspired by Taoist writings, perfectly express the spirit of Lee's revolutionary methodology.

> How can there be methods and systems to arrive at something that is living? To that which is static, fixed, dead, there can be a way, a definite path, but not to that which is living. Do not reduce reality to a static thing and then invent methods to reach it. (Lee 1975)

> True observation begins when one sheds set patterns, and true freedom of expression occurs when one is beyond systems. (Lee 1971)

> *Knowledge* is fixed in time, whereas, *knowing* is continual. Knowledge comes from a source, from accumulation, from a conclusion, while knowing is a movement. (Lee 1975)

> Jeet Kune Do favors formlessness so that it can assume all forms and since Jeet Kune Do has no style, it can fit with all styles. As a result, Jeet Kune Do utilizes all ways and is bound by none and, likewise, uses any techniques or means which serve its ends (Ibidem)

As can be grasped from these sentences, rather than being an organized system, Lee's Jeet Kune Do was meant to be a laboratory where fighting theories and techniques could be put to the test. Students could experiment with them without being bound to follow any unless they wished to. The words written around the very symbol of JKD stand as the catchy slogan for Lee's methodology, "Using no way as the way; having no limitation as limitation." (Little 1996)

Shortly after Lee's death, Paul K. Feyerabend, one of the most provocative Western philosophers of the last part of the twentieth century, came out with an intriguing book destined to shake the scientific and philosophical establishment of the day. The book, appropriately entitled *Against Method,* is a manifesto applying to science the same ideas expressed by Lee in the field of martial arts (Feyerabend 1975). In the book, Feyerabend does nothing less than attack the Cartesian method on which most of Western science is built. Arguing that most scientists, in their blind devotion to a particularly restrictive methodology, lack the flexibility necessary for truly open-minded scientific inquiry, Feyerabend echoes Lee's sentiments about classical martial artists. Both men, in fact, unequivocally state that the strict observance of any particular methodology inhibits intuition, represses individuality and closes people's minds rather than opening them. Worse yet, these methodologies are too limited by their own rules to be able to grasp anything more than small, partial truths. What both Lee and Feyerabend advocated in place of such a hopelessly rigid mindset was epistemological anarchism.

Acknowledging that any method possesses strengths as well as weaknesses, epistemological anarchism is an extremely open-minded approach willing to adopt any method showing promise for delivering the desired results. Because of this, epistemological anarchism utilizes a method's strengths without being bound by its weaknesses. Just as Taoism argued that rules are necessary only for those who are too stupid to make the right choice on their own, epistemological anarchism holds that absolute laws are an obstacle to genuine understanding. Whereas guidelines can be useful, absolute laws limit the individual's flexibility to decide what is appropriate in each situation.

Clearly, such freedom is not for everyone. As Confucianism recognized, when left free, stupid people are bound to make stupid choices, and for this reason it is important that they follow laws guiding their behavior. However, epistemological anarchists, along with Taoists would probably agree with William Blake when he said, "One Law for the Lion and Ox is Oppression" (Blake 1975). Absolute laws end up being nothing but prisons for individuals with acute minds and powerful visions. It is with these individuals in mind that, as a corollary to the idea of "using no way as the way," the epistemological anarchism advocated by Lee (with which, no doubt, Feyerabend agreed) articulated its own very open four-step methodology.

1. Research your own experience.
2. Absorb what is useful.
3. Reject what is useless.
4. Add what is specifically your own. (Little 1996)

Through this set of prepositions, Lee gave full power back to the individual. Epistemological anarchism, in fact, does not attempt to substitute one method with another. Rather, it frees individuals to find their own methods, and invites them to change them at will if, after some time, their discovery stops producing the desired results.

In *Thus Spoke Zarathustra,* Nietzsche wrote a splendid declaration of epistemological anarchism, "'This is my way; where is yours?'—thus I answered those who asked me 'the way.' For *the* way—that does not exist." (Nietzsche 1995). Buddha himself invited his followers to find out the truth for themselves without depending on anything or anyone, not even on his teachings (Smith 1991). In a similar spirit, Lee wrote, " ... jeet kune do is merely a term, a label to be used as a boat to get across: once across, it is to be discarded and not carried on one's back." (Lee 1971). In this way, Lee resisted the temptation to turn his own intuition into dogma, downplayed his own self-importance as a teacher, and encouraged people to make up their own theories and become their own teachers. In fact, the essence of the epistemological anarchism that he espoused was in creating one's own method by taking bits and pieces from different sources, and recombining them into a new format.

SIMPLICITY

Although the key words of Lee's "non-method" are creativity, flexibility and synthesis, he recognized the danger of unchecked experimentation. Being willing to take ideas from different sources, the JKD martial artist may end up overwhelmed by an overload of information and unable to utilize the tools at her/his disposal in a meaningful way. Rather than being bound to one method, the JKD fighter gets lost in a myriad of different ideas and techniques. Always rejecting traditional methods can also turn into a new type dogma. Worse yet, the JKD martial artist may become so infatuated with the technical variety offered by the process of picking and choosing from different sources as to turn into a collector. In this way, she/he effectively trades one prison for another. The lack of boundaries becomes as paralyzing as the oppressiveness of too many rules. Too many choices can lead astray those who are unable to choose what is useful and what is not.

In order to avoid this mistake, Lee again turned to Taoism. A few thousands years before Lee's time, Lao Tzu had written, "Learning consists in daily accumulating; the practice of Tao consists in daily diminishing." (Lao Tzu 1989) Following this lead, Lee came up with a rule of thumb designed to warn against the mistake of useless accumulation. In one of his most quoted statements, he reminded his followers that "The height of cultivation runs to simplicity." (Lee 1975)

Since Lao Tzu's poetry does not waste time on explanations, in order to clear up this concept, Lee used an illustration popularized by Zen Buddhism. According to this doctrine, knowledge comes in three stages. Before any kind of learning takes place, people are ignorant, and therefore simple. When they begin learning, they shed their ignorance, become sophisticated and aware of the subtle complexities of life. At this stage, they turn into very complex, intellectual beings. Their knowledge is vast but weighs them down. Spontaneity and innocence are lost in exchange for this knowledge. For many people, this is the end of the journey. The knowledge they have accumulated separates them from the simple, ignorant people, and therefore they go on accumulating more and more. This is the mistake of many intellectuals and is also the mistake of JKD followers infatuated with variety. Zen and Taoism, on the other hand, take a different route. They let go of the heavy, excess intellectual baggage they have accumulated and return to simplicity. However, there is a deep difference between the initial simplicity of ignorance and the kind of simplicity they search. The first lacks knowledge. The second has acquired knowledge, but has moved beyond accumulation and is not weighed down by it. It was after this deep, rich kind of simplicity, and not after accumulation, that Lee urged his followers to direct their energies.

PHILOSOPHY GOES TO THE MOVIES (AND SPILLS POPCORN ALL OVER ITSELF)

All of the basic principles of Lee's philosophy that have been analyzed in this chapter can be found in a variety of written sources: Lee's own books, books written about him, interviews, articles, and even some of the notes that he left behind. However, considering that Lee gained worldwide fame mainly as an actor, any discussion of Lee's philosophy that did not at least briefly address how the philosophy played into his movies would be incomplete. In order to fill this gap, let us now turn to how Lee's ideas appeared (or did not) in his movies.

Generally speaking, movies are not the best form of media to convey philosophical ideas. Martial arts movies, in particular, are not exactly famous for their philosophical depth. Fast-paced action scenes and spectacular stunts are the staple of this genre in which the plot is often little more than a pretext for the fighting sequences. Since audiences usually do not watch martial arts movies for their fine intellectual content, producers often save on the unnecessary expenditure of a decent screenwriter by recycling the same plot over and over. In these movies, the gods presiding over the destiny of the hero's family members must be on a permanent vacation, for they always end up killed, maimed or otherwise injured. The typical plot, in fact, runs like this: the hero of the story happily minds his own business and is reluctant to fight until forced to act by the Bad Guy who kidnaps, and/or insults, and/or kills, and/or rapes, and/or tortures the hero's teacher, lover, parent, grandparent, or family pet, thereby giving the hero an excuse to seek revenge. At that point, the hero is either forced to join the inevitable, deadly martial arts tournament organized by the Bad Guy, or simply turns from a perfect candidate for the Nobel Peace Prize into a killing machine which does not stop until he gets revenge during the final, cathartic fight with the Evil One.

Bruce Lee's movies, being the model for the genre, do not escape the above description. From tournaments to murdered loved ones, Lee's four movies (five if we include the posthumous *Game of Death*) contain all the defining elements of martial arts films. Philosophy, on the other hand, seems to be (literally) missing in action. For example, in order to find any sign of philosophical life in Lee's first two movies, *Fist of Fury* and *The Chinese Connection* (a.k.a. *The Big Boss*), one needs the gift of a very fertile imagination. As an explanation for this complete lack of philosophical substance in the works of a man who was so immersed in philosophy, we need to remember that in 1971 Lee was still not particularly famous as an actor. For this reason, it is logical to assume that he did not have much power to influence the scripts of the first two movies. In fact, as soon as Lee gained great fame, philosophy entered into his films. In his next (and last) two movies, *Return of the Dragon* and *Enter the Dragon,* glimpses of Lee's philosophy manage to come out in between action sequences.

In *Return of the Dragon,* Lee's opposition to ideological dogmatism comes out in a friendly argument with a fellow Chinese. In this brief dialogue, Lee scoffs at his friend's patriotic refusal to study karate on the ground that it is a foreign art. To his friend's closed-minded patriotism, Lee offers an open approach willing to "take what is useful" from any available source. Although the dialogue is hardly enlightening, it provides a quick example of Lee's attempt to introduce deeper themes in his movies.

In the final fight of *Return of the Dragon,* Lee again inserts a small philosophical element. Like all movie heroes, Lee begins the fight by losing. At this point, however, unlike the heroes of other movies, who usually rely only on willpower to come back and win, Lee changes his fighting style to suit the situation. Lee's opponent, on the other hand, is bound to only one form of fighting and is therefore unable to change. This lack of flexibility proves fatal and Lee goes on to soundly defeat his opponent. In this scene, the Taoist emphasis on being able to change to suit the circumstances and on having no form in order to be able to assume all forms are the keys allowing Lee to win what started out as an unfavorable fight: a perfect application of the principles of Jeet Kune Do.

If in *Return of the Dragon* Lee timidly began introducing philosophical themes, in *Enter the Dragon* he added more philosophical fuel to the fire. The very beginning of the movie sees Lee is in a temple teaching martial arts to a young pupil. In this dialogue, Lee uses plenty of Zen sayings (a paraphrase of the famous "The wise man points at the moon, but the fool looks at the finger") and stresses Zen ideas such as relying on intuition more than on abstract rationality. Just a few minutes later, Lee re-enacts a notorious samurai story about "the art of fighting without fighting." Faithfully following the Japanese story, which is said to be based on a historical event, Lee has his character on a ship in the company of an arrogant martial artist looking to practice his skills on the passengers. When the martial artist rudely asks what style he practices, Lee answers;

"You can call it the art of fighting without fighting." Lee then proceeds to accept the ensuing challenge on one condition. Since his style cannot be properly performed in a tight space, the match is to take place on a nearby island. Eager to fight, the challenger accepts and jumps on to a small lifeboat. Immediately, Lee pushes the lifeboat away from the ship, thereby getting rid of the obnoxious challenger without having to fight. After this splendid demonstration of philosophy applied to fighting, the rest of *Enter the Dragon* gives way to the familiar cliches that make up most martial arts movies. Apparently, Lee had planned to include more philosophical material, but those scenes were cut for fear of being too complicated for the audience (Little 1996).

More evidence of Lee's wish to include philosophy in his films can be found in a movie in which Lee did not act at all. Based on a story written by Lee and by some of his famous students (actor James Coburn and screenwriter Stirling Silliphant), *Circle of Iron* (aka *The Silent Flute*) is perhaps the most anomalous martial arts movie ever made. In fact, whereas the fighting sequences are of extremely poor quality, the philosophical effort is commendable. References to Heraclitus, Buddhist and Taoist ideas fill a plot based around a search for wisdom and self-knowledge. Although the quality of the work can be debated, *Circle of Iron* is certainly a courageous project and a manifesto of Lee's own philosophy. The dedication made to Lee at the beginning of the film clearly points to Lee's desire to make philosophy a big part of his movies:

> Prior to the death of the legendary Bruce Lee, he helped to create a movie story that might capture not only the spirit of martial arts, but a part of the spirit of the Zen philosophy he lived by. He was aware that a film with these dynamics would cause controversy, particularly among those unfamiliar with Zen beliefs. But it was this very uniqueness that he believed would enthrall the moviegoer.... It is to Bruce Lee that this film is posthumously dedicated (*Circle of Iron* 1979)

Although as we can see from the paucity of these examples, Lee's films were hardly full of philosophical dialogues, we can also see how, as Lee gained fame and influence, philosophy gained a more prominent role in each new movie. Had Lee's life and acting career not met such a premature end, it seems safe to assume that Lee would have used his growing popularity to make philosophy a much more central part of his pictures. Had that happened, perhaps the entire genre of martial arts movies would have taken a different turn. Although I have a difficult time imagining Van Damme starring in Zen scripts (again my apologies to Van Damme for picking on him) and although I doubt that many people would pay to watch martial arts movies with little violence and much philosophy, Lee's early death leaves us with many unanswered questions about what might have been.

JEET KUNE DO AS THE ARCHETYPAL MARTIAL ART OF THE 1960S

The importance of the context in which ideas came to light is sometimes downplayed in the study of philosophy. For example, if most of Lee's philosophy is derived from Asian sources that are thousands of years old, one may guess that the context in which Lee lived did not contribute much to the articulation of his philosophy. The assumption is logical but, as logic often goes, terribly wrong.

In its philosophical outlook, in fact, Jeet Kune Do is the quintessential martial art of the 1960s. It is not simply because the 1960s were the decade in which Lee came up with the main concepts of his new approach to martial arts. Rather, Jeet Kune Do is the embodiment in martial arts form of many of the wild, revolutionary ideas that characterized the sixties. If we attempt the impossible task of imagining JKD being created and popularized in a more conformist cultural context such as that existing in the 1950s, we can immediately see how Lee's art is irremediably tied to the extreme, passionate spirit of the American West Coast in the 1960s. Can any of us picture Lee's ideas being well received in South Dakota in, let's say, 1952? Forget becoming a popular hero. With his anti-patriotic, anti-organized religion, antiauthoritarian, liberal ideas, Lee would have been lucky not to have been lynched as soon as he opened his mouth.

In any context other than the sixties, Lee would have been accused of being an ungrateful flag-burner and invited to quickly go back where he came from. As Giordano Bruno and thousands of people tried for heresy and witchery could attest, many times in history people have been burned at the stake for much milder criticisms of established authority. In most places and during most centuries, Lee's libertarian views would have been considered an intolerable threat by the religious and/or political powers of the day, and would have been immediately and severely dealt with.

In the sixties, however, it was a completely different story. Both those people who loved and those who hated the 1960s agree that they probably were the most tumultuous decade of the twentieth century and that they have drastically altered American consciousness and beliefs. Politically, it was the time of the antiwar movement and the civil rights movement. It was the time when hundreds of organizations radically opposed to the government sprung up like mushrooms. Culturally, thousands of people became disillusioned with the Euro-centric view that Western culture was the best of all, and began looking for answers elsewhere. Asian religions and philosophies gained instant popularity. Traditional values were questioned and criticized. "Question Authority"—a concept that Lee particularly loved—became one of the favorite slogans of the decade. The sexual revolution shocked the Puritan values that, up until that point, had ruled the attitude of most Americans toward sexuality. Free, uninhibited experimentation with anything, from drugs to ideology, was openly practiced. From music to cinematography, all forms of art experienced an incredible boost of creativity. It was a decade of fast, extreme change. The air was filled with the sense of possibility.

At a time when no forms of established authority went unchallenged, it seems only natural that even the field of martial arts was destined to experience some drastic change. It was in this receptive context that Lee stepped up with his radical form of Taoism and Zen. Lee's highly unconventional personal background (an interracial marriage with a young white woman, his willingness to teach anyone regardless of ethnicity, the match fought against a Chinese martial artist sent to stop Lee from divulging martial arts "secrets" to non-Chinese, the fact that he had never received a formal teaching license) united with his equally unconventional philosophy and his public role as an actor allowed him to become the man who was to take the spirit of the sixties into the martial arts world. The philosophy of JKD can therefore be seen as the gift (or the curse, depending on your point of view) of the alchemical mixing of Taoism, Zen Buddhism, the antiauthoritarian culture of the 1960s, and Bruce Lee's own personality. Regardless of whether we agree with Lee's approach or not, his example remains as an open invitation to do one of the healthiest things that anyone, martial artist or not, can do; questioning one's own beliefs.

References

Blake, William. *The Marriage of Heaven and Hell*. London and New York: Oxford University Press, 1975.

Cartmell, Tim. "Martial Arts Revolutionary: Wang Xiang Zhai Part I". *Journal of Chinese Martial Arts*. Clearwater (FL): pp. 3–5, March-April 1998, Vol. 3 #14.

Cartmell, Tim. "Martial Arts Revolutionary: Wang Xiang Zhai Part II". *Journal of Chinese Martial Arts*. Clearwater (FL): pp. 15–16, July-August 1998, Vol. 3 #16.

Chuang Tzu. *The Complete Works of Chuang-Tzu*. (transl. Burton Watson) New York: Columbia University Press, 1968.

Donohue, John J. *Warrior Dreams: The Martial Arts and the American Imagination*. Westport: Bergin & Garvey, 1994.

Feyerabend, Paul K. *Against Method: Outline of an Anarchist Theory of Knowledge*. Atlantic Highlands (NJ): Humanities Press, 1975.

Heraclitus, of Ephesus. *The Cosmic Fragments*. (ed. G.S. Kirk) Cambridge (England): University Press, 1975.

Krishnamurti, Jiddu. *The Collected Works of Krishnamurti*. San Francisco: Harper and Row, 1980.

Krishnamurti, Jiddu. *The First and Last Freedom.* New York: Harper, 1954.

Krishnamurti, Jiddu. *The Only Revolution.* New York: Harper and Row, 1970.

Lao Tzu. *Tao Te Ching.* (transl. John C.H. Woo) Boston: Shambala Dragon Editions, 1989.

Lee, Bruce. *The Tao of Jeet Kune Do.* Santa Clarita: Ohara Publications, 1975.

Lee, Bruce. "Liberate Yourself from Classical Karate. In *Black Belt* magazine[September, 1971].

Little, John. *The Warrior Within.* Lincolnwood: Contemporary Books, 1996.

Maciocia, Giovanni. *The Foundations of Chinese Medicine: A Comprehensive Text for Acupuncturists and Herbalists.* New York: Churchill Livingstone, 1989.

Maliszewski, Michael. *Spiritual Dimensions of the Martial Arts.* Rutland: Charles E. Tuttle Company, 1996.

Miller, Dan. "The Origins of Pa Kua Chang: Part II" *Pa Kua Chang Journal.* Pacific Grove (CA): High View Publications, vol. 3 #2, January/February 1993.

Miller, Dan. "Martial Arts Taught in the Old Tradition (Part II): The Deterioration of the Complete Martial Arts System". *Pa Kua Chang Journal.* Pacific Grove (CA): High View Publications, vol. 4 #5, July/August 1994.

Nietzsche, Friedrich. *Thus Spoke Zarathustra.* (transl. Walter Kaufmann) New York: Random House, 1995.

Robbins, Tom. *Another Roadside Attraction.* New York: Bantam Books, 1971.

Smith, Huston. *The World's Religions.* San Francisco: HarperSanFrancisco, 1991 [1958].

Trungpa, Chogyam. *Shambala: The Sacred Path of the Warrior.* Boston: Shambala Dragon Editions, 1988.

Wheelwright, Philip. *Heraclitus.* New York: Oxford University Press, 1959.

Wright, Arthur F. *Buddhism in Chinese History.* Stanford: Stanford University Press, 1959.